Building Peace

Moving seamlessly from the global to the local, from the politics of institutions to the theoretical apparatus through which we analyse peace and security governance, the contributions to this volume draw attention to the operations of gendered power in peacebuilding across diverse contexts and explore the possibilities of gender-sensitive, sustainable peace. The authors have wide-ranging expertise in gendered analysis of the peacebuilding practices of international and national organisations, detailed and complex qualitative analysis of the gendered politics of peacebuilding in specific country contexts, and feminist analysis of the tools we use to think with when approaching contemporary debates about peacebuilding. The volume thus serves not only as a useful marker of the development of feminist encounters with peacebuilding but also as a foundation for future scholarship in this area.

This book was originally published as a special issue of the journal *Peacebuilding*.

Laura J. Shepherd is Associate Professor of International Relations at UNSW Australia (University of New South Wales), and a Visiting Senior Fellow in the Centre for Women, Peace and Security at the London School of Economics and Political Science, UK. Her primary research engages the motifs of participation and protection that characterise debates about women, peace and security in global politics.

Building Peace
Feminist Perspectives

Edited by
Laura J. Shepherd

LONDON AND NEW YORK

First published 2017
by Routledge
2 Park Square, Milton Park, Abingdon, Oxon, OX14 4RN, UK

and by Routledge
711 Third Avenue, New York, NY 10017, USA

Routledge is an imprint of the Taylor & Francis Group, an informa business

© 2017 Taylor & Francis

All rights reserved. No part of this book may be reprinted or reproduced
or utilised in any form or by any electronic, mechanical, or other means,
now known or hereafter invented, including photocopying and recording,
or in any information storage or retrieval system, without permission in
writing from the publishers.

Trademark notice: Product or corporate names may be trademarks or
registered trademarks, and are used only for identification and
explanation without intent to infringe.

British Library Cataloguing in Publication Data
A catalogue record for this book is available from the British Library

ISBN 13: 978-0-415-79181-6

Typeset in Minion Pro
by RefineCatch Limited, Bungay, Suffolk

Publisher's Note
The publisher accepts responsibility for any inconsistencies that may have
arisen during the conversion of this book from journal articles to book chapters,
namely the possible inclusion of journal terminology.

Disclaimer
Every effort has been made to contact copyright holders for their permission to
reprint material in this book. The publishers would be grateful to hear from any
copyright holder who is not here acknowledged and will undertake to rectify
any errors or omissions in future editions of this book.

Contents

Citation Information	vii
Notes on Contributors	ix

1. Victims of violence or agents of change? Representations of women in UN peacebuilding discourse — 1
   Laura J. Shepherd

2. A seat at the table is not enough: understanding women's substantive representation in peace processes — 16
   Kara Ellerby

3. The relationship of political settlement analysis to peacebuilding from a feminist perspective — 31
   Fionnuala Ní Aoláin

4. Light, heat and shadows: women's reflections on peacebuilding in post-conflict Bougainville — 46
   Nicole George

5. 'What is wrong with men?': revisiting violence against women in conflict and peacebuilding — 59
   Donna Pankhurst

6. Decolonising gender and peacebuilding: feminist frontiers and border thinking in Africa — 73
   Heidi Hudson

7. Feminists building peace and reconciliation: beyond post-conflict — 89
   Elisabeth Porter

Index — 105

Citation Information

The chapters in this book were originally published in *Peacebuilding*, volume 4, issue 2 (June 2016). When citing this material, please use the original page numbering for each article, as follows:

Chapter 1
Victims of violence or agents of change? Representations of women in UN peacebuilding discourse
Laura J. Shepherd
Peacebuilding, volume 4, issue 2 (June 2016), pp. 121–135

Chapter 2
A seat at the table is not enough: understanding women's substantive representation in peace processes
Kara Ellerby
Peacebuilding, volume 4, issue 2 (June 2016), pp. 136–150

Chapter 3
The relationship of political settlement analysis to peacebuilding from a feminist perspective
Fionnuala Ní Aoláin
Peacebuilding, volume 4, issue 2 (June 2016), pp. 151–165

Chapter 4
Light, heat and shadows: women's reflections on peacebuilding in post-conflict Bougainville
Nicole George
Peacebuilding, volume 4, issue 2 (June 2016), pp. 166–179

Chapter 5
'What is wrong with men?': revisiting violence against women in conflict and peacebuilding
Donna Pankhurst
Peacebuilding, volume 4, issue 2 (June 2016), pp. 180–193

Chapter 6
Decolonising gender and peacebuilding: feminist frontiers and border thinking in Africa
Heidi Hudson
Peacebuilding, volume 4, issue 2 (June 2016), pp. 194–209

CITATION INFORMATION

Chapter 7
Feminists building peace and reconciliation: beyond post-conflict
Elisabeth Porter
Peacebuilding, volume 4, issue 2 (June 2016), pp. 210–225

For any permission-related enquiries please visit:
http://www.tandfonline.com/page/help/permissions

Notes on Contributors

Fionnuala Ní Aoláin holds the Robina Chair in Law, Public Policy and Society at the University of Minnesota Law School, USA, and is concurrently a Professor of Law and Associate Director at Ulster University's Transitional Justice Institute, Belfast, Ireland.

Kara Ellerby is Assistant Professor in the Department of Political Science and International Relations at the University of Delaware, USA, with a joint appointment in Women and Gender Studies. Her research interests include global gender norms, gender and security, African post-conflict peacebuilding and feminist international relations.

Nicole George is Senior Lecturer in Peace and Conflict Studies in the School of Political Science and International Studies at the University of Queensland, Australia. Her research is focused on gender, violence, peacebuilding and conflict transition in the Pacific Islands.

Heidi Hudson is Professor of International Relations and Director of the Centre for Africa Studies at the University of the Free State, Bloemfontein, South Africa. She is a global fellow of the Peace Research Institute Oslo (PRIO) and co-editor of the *International Feminist Journal of Politics*.

Donna Pankhurst is Professor in Peace Studies, University of Bradford, UK. She has a history of research and teaching in the areas of gender, conflict and development – particularly focusing on Africa. In recent years, she has been analysing gender-based violence in so-called post-conflict contexts, with an increasing focus on men, and explanations for why they commit acts of violence against women.

Elisabeth Porter is Professor of International Relations at the University of South Australia and has a range of teaching responsibilities, including a course on peace, justice and reconciliation. Her most recent books include *Connecting Peace, Justice and Reconciliation* (Lynne Rienner, 2015).

Laura J. Shepherd is Associate Professor of International Relations in the School of Social Sciences at UNSW Australia. Laura is author/editor of six books, including *Gender Matters in Global Politics* (Routledge, 2nd edn, 2015) and *Gender, Violence and Popular Culture: Telling Stories* (Routledge, 2013).

Victims of violence or agents of change? Representations of women in UN peacebuilding discourse

Laura J. Shepherd

School of Social Sciences, UNSW Australia, Sydney, Australia

ABSTRACT
The Women, Peace and Security agenda at the United Nations is the policy architecture that assures the meaningful participation of women in UN peacebuilding and post-conflict reconstruction activities. It is a reasonable expectation that UN entities would leverage WPS principles and priorities to inform gender-responsive peacebuilding and recovery. This paper investigates the imbrication of WPS discourse in the discourse of the UN Peacebuilding Commission. I argue that there has historically been limited integration of the WPS architecture with the UN PBC, but this does not mean that the Commission's activities are not upholding and even enhancing WPS principles and objectives. The opposite is true, and this raises interesting questions about the coherence of the WPS agenda, and the UN as an organisation, in terms of its ability to develop and implement an integrated and holistic gender-sensitive peacebuilding agenda.

UN Security Council Resolution (UNSCR) 1325, adopted in 2000, is the first of eight resolutions addressing the gender dynamics of peacemaking, peacebuilding, and international peace and security; all eight resolutions are binding on all UN member states and other UN entities.[1] The resolution articulates three priority issues: the *prevention* of violence, particularly sexualised and gender-based violence; the meaningful *participation* of women in peace and security governance; and the *protection* of women's rights and bodies in conflict and post-conflict situations. This and subsequent resolutions form the architecture of the Women, Peace and Security (WPS) agenda at the United Nations, the title of which is drawn from the listed title of UNSCR 1325; the WPS agenda guides women's participation and mandates the application of a 'gender lens'[2] to all aspects of peace and conflict.

To understand what is expected of women, and what is expected of both the international community and state actors in the context of gender-responsive peace and security governance, it is necessary to understand how these resolutions represent women. It is

---

[1]The policy architecture of the agenda consists of eight UN Security Council resolutions published under the title of 'Women and Peace and Security'. These resolutions are UNSCR 1325 (2000); UNSCR 1820 (2008); UNSCR 1888 (2009); UNSCR 1889 (2009); UNSCR 1960 (2010); UNSCR 2106 (2013); UNSCR 2122 (2013); and UNSCR 2242 (2015).

[2]Anne Sisson Runyan and V. Spike Peterson, *Global Gender Issues in the New Millennium* (Boulder, CO: Westview, 2014), 5–8.

also important to understand how these resolutions guide practices of peace and security governance, by investigating whether the principles enshrined in the WPS agenda have spread from the UN Security Council to other UN entities. Here, I analyse discourse about peacebuilding-related activities undertaken under the auspices of the UN. This research presented in this article was guided by two central questions: What are the different constructions of women, and representations of gender, that emerge in UN peacebuilding discourse? And, to what extent are WPS principles and obligations manifest in peacebuilding discourse? I compiled two sets of discursive artefacts to serve as the data for the investigation. These data consist of a number of interviews I conducted at various UN offices in New York in 2013 and 2014 and a selection of documents from the archives of the UN Peacebuilding Commission (PBC), all of which are available online:[3] statements from the Chair (11/10/2006–21/07/2015), and the documentation produced by the Working Group on Lessons Learned (WGLL) (20/02/2007–20/10/2015).[4] I draw the documentation from the UN PBC as this is the entity formally associated with peacebuilding in the UN system.

The interview data were generated during two periods of field research in New York, during which I was able to meet with many individuals, and some teams, involved in the UN's peacebuilding-related activities. Interviews were mostly unstructured and lasted approximately an hour each, producing 163 pages of transcribed data. This article draws on the five interviews with research participants that spoke most directly to the themes addressed in this article, comprising approximately one-third of the total corpus. These interviews are simply numbered in the analysis below. All research participants agreed to speak to me on the grounds that I would provide full anonymity for them, extending to their institutional affiliation, hence the data analysed here is attributed anonymously, with no mention of institutional location.

The sets of documents were selected for inclusion on the basis of their applicability to the questions I wish to explore here. The Chair of the Peacebuilding Commission is the 'public face' of the institution, and his statements (the Chair, thus far, has always been male) at the commencement and conclusion of his term of office address the core priorities and goals of the Commission at the time.[5] It is useful to interrogate these statements, then, to investigate whether the Women, Peace and Security resolutions are referenced at all, and whether mention is made, for example, of gender-sensitive peacebuilding as an institutional priority. The priorities of the Working Group on Lessons Learned reflect areas where the Commission perceives either a deficit in its knowledge base or a 'hot topic' relevant to the in-country management of peacebuilding-related activities. The extent to which the outcome documentation of the discussions conducted under the auspices of the Working Group discusses Women, Peace and Security principles is of direct relevance to the questions that guide this research. Moreover, given the function of the Working Group – to translate and transmit peacebuilding knowledge drawn from a range of different contexts

---

[3] All documentation is available at http://www.un.org/en/peacebuilding/st_chair.shtml and http://www.un.org/en/peacebuilding/doc_lessonslearned.shtml.

[4] In total, I analysed 131 documents in the course of this part of the research: 40 statements from the Chair and 91 documents from the WGLL. This article presents findings drawn from a larger project investigating logics of gender and space in UN peacebuilding discourse. In the course of the larger project, I analysed hundreds of documents produced by or related to the UN Peacebuilding Commission, including Organisational Committee records, historical documents and the formal and informal records of the country-specific configurations, as well as those cited here.

[5] The Chair is chosen by the Organisational Committee (OC), which in turn consists of 31 UN member states. Further information is available at http://www.un.org/en/peacebuilding/pbso/faq.shtml (accessed January 5, 2016).

to practitioners working under the auspices of the UN – the types of knowledge about women and gender-sensitive peacebuilding that is represented is of key significance to this investigation.

I begin by locating my research in the literature on women in peacebuilding, exploring the ways in which scholarship on peacebuilding and peace and security more broadly has engaged with the representation of women. I then explore the ways in which 'women' are differently represented in peacebuilding discourse at the UN. I argue that there has historically been very limited direct integration of the WPS architecture in peacebuilding discourse (which would be evidenced, for example, by explicit mention of the WPS resolutions, or reference to the Women, Peace and Security agenda or principles). Instead, peacebuilding discourse tends to focus on the UN Secretary-General's 2010 report on women in peacebuilding and the concomitant seven-point Action Plan as its guide to gender-responsive peacebuilding. This report, and the Action Plan itself, can reasonably be conceptualised as part of the broader WPS architecture, but these documents are not conventionally seen as 'WPS canon'. It is important to note, however, that just because the research participants whose speech I analyse here did not *ever* mention the Women, Peace and Security agenda directly, this does not mean that their activities are not upholding and even enhancing WPS principles and objectives. I identify the construction of women as 'agents of change', while also laying out the ways in which peacebuilding discourse seems to constitute agency primarily as economic agency rather than political agency. I argue that women's participation in peacebuilding seems to be strongly tied to their subjectivity as economic agents, but that the persistent representation of women as 'agents of change' at least creates an association between the subject of 'woman' and the concept of 'agency' that potentially could create positive horizons of possibility for women involved in peacebuilding-related activities under the auspices of the UN.

Victims of violence or agents of change: women in peacebuilding

Feminist scholars of peacebuilding have highlighted not only that the individuals involved in peacebuilding and other forms of peace and security activity are embodied – and gendered – subjects, but also that policies aimed at facilitating peacebuilding rely on concepts, including the concept of 'peace' itself, which are inherently gendered.[6] Such scholarship has noted that early engagements with the gendered dynamics of conflict 'tended to portray a simplistic division of roles: men were the perpetrators … while women were the victims' of violence.[7] But, as Carol Cohn has more recently summarised, gendered realities of war are 'far more complex than this old story portrays. War itself is more complexly gendered than this masculinized story allows, and women's role in and experience of war is far more integral and varied'.[8] Consistently representing women as 'victims of violence' curtails their agency and precludes the development of appropriate peacebuilding-related activities that

---

[6]For an overview of this literature, see Caitlin Hamilton and Laura J. Shepherd, 'Gender and Peacebuilding', in *Handbook of Gender and War*, eds. Simona Sharoni et al. (London: Edward Elgar, 2016).

[7]Caroline O. N. Moser and Fiona C. Clark, 'Introduction', in *Victims, Perpetrators or Actors? Gender, Armed Conflict and Political Violence*, eds. Caroline O. N. Moser and Fiona C. Clark (London: Zed, 2001), 3.

[8]Carol Cohn, 'Women and Wars: Towards a Conceptual Framework', in *Women & Wars*, ed. Carol Cohn (Cambridge: Polity Press, 2013), 1.

address the full spectrum of women's experiences during conflict and in the post-conflict environment.[9]

It is not as simple, however, as reversing the discursive logics such that women as peace-building subjects are ascribed agency in peacebuilding discourse. Much has also been written about the politics of representing women as 'agents of change' in peacebuilding-related activities, insofar as it risks reinscribing a link between femininity and peace that relies on essentialist notions of what it means to be a woman and how by virtue of their femininity (their nurturing abilities) women are better able to work towards peaceful resolutions to conflict.[10] These essentialisms have been strategically deployed in pursuit of creating access points for women to discussion and decision-making in peacebuilding activities,[11] but this is not without its challenges. As Cynthia Cockburn has noted, 'essentialism is a dangerous political force, designed to shore up differences and inequalities, to sustain dominations. It operates through stereotypes that fix identities in eternal dualisms: woman victim, man warrior'.[12] Feminist scholarship on women in peacebuilding draws attention to the multiple, various, roles that they play and, while acknowledging that we should not expect 'more from women (super heroines) than we expect of men' *just because they are women*,[13] demonstrates exactly what is overlooked if women are not included in analysis of peacebuilding practice.[14]

Institutionally, women have not been systematically included in the practices of peace-building either. A decade ago, Hilary Charlesworth noted that '[t]he need to involve women in peace-building is regularly ignored by the UN and other international institutions', citing Sanam Anderlini's indictment of 'the UN's "Triple-A" syndrome with respect to women and peace: apathy, ad hoc practices and amnesia'.[15] More recently, a team of researchers led by Radhika Coomaraswamy undertook a global study 'to assess progress at the global, regional and national levels in implementing resolution 1325';[16] the report was published in 2015 to inform the high-level review that took place in the same year.[17] Several chapters in the report focus on women's participation in peace processes and the importance of women's representation in peacebuilding-related activities. The report found that 27% of peace agreements since 2000 have made reference to women, more than double the 1990–2000 level.[18] Given that the recognition of women in peace agreements is an integral component of the Women, Peace and Security agenda, the increase in the proportion of agreements that

---

[9]See Caroline O. N. Moser and Fiona C. Clark, eds., *Victims, Perpetrators or Actors? Gender, Armed Conflict and Political Violence* (London: Zed, 2001); Inger Skjelsbæk and Dan Smith, eds., *Gender, Peace and Conflict* (London: Sage, 2001); and Laura J. Shepherd, *Gender, Violence and Security: Discourse as Practice* (London: Zed, 2008).

[10]See Hilary Charlesworth, 'Are Women Peaceful? Reflections on the Role of Women in Peacebuilding', *Feminist Legal Studies* 16: 347–61; Sanam N. Anderlini, *Women Building Peace: What They Do, Why it Matters* (Boulder, CO: Lynne Rienner, 2007); Laura J. Shepherd, 'Sex, Security and Superhero(in)es: From 1325 to 1820 and Beyond', *International Feminist Journal of Politics* 13, no. 4 (2011): 504–21; Laura J. Shepherd, 'Gender and Global Social Justice: Peacebuilding and the Politics of Participation', in *Global Social Justice*, eds. Heather Widdows and Nicola J. Smith (London: Routledge, 2011), 128–37; Malathi de Alwis, Julie Mertus and Tazreena Sajjad, 'Women and Peace Processes', in *Women & Wars*, ed. Carol Cohn (Cambridge: Polity Press, 2013), 169–93.

[11]Anderlini, *Women Building Peace*, 197.

[12]Cynthia Cockburn, *The Space between Us: Negotiating Gender and National Identities in Conflict* (London: Zed, 1998): 13.

[13]Carol Cohn, Helen Kinsella and Sheri Gibbings, 'Women, Peace and Security: Resolution 1325', *International Feminist Journal of Politics* 6, no. 1 (2004): 136.

[14]See, for example, Anderlini, *Women Building Peace*; Elisabeth Porter, *Peacebuilding: Women in International Perspective* (London: Routledge, 2007); and Donna Pankhurst, ed. *Gendered Peace: Women's Struggles for Post-war Justice and Reconciliation* (London: Routledge, 2008).

[15]Charlesworth, 'Are Women Peaceful?' 358–9.

[16]United Nations Security Council, 'Resolution 2122', S/RES/2122 (2013), OP 15.

[17]Radhika Coomaraswamy et al., *Preventing Conflict, Transforming Peace, Securing the Peace: A Global Study on the Implementation of United Nations Security Council Resolution 1325* (New York: UN Women, 2015).

[18]Coomaraswamy et al., *Preventing Conflict*, 44.

reference women is a welcome change. This does not necessarily correlate with increased numbers of women in mediation or peace negotiations, however, nor does it mean that careful consideration is given to how women's interest can best be represented. As the report comments, '[t]he present programmes put forward by the international community tend to be extremely narrow: just to bring a female body to the table'.[19]

I am not able to resolve the tensions in the representations of women in peacebuilding any more than I am able to resolve the issue of women's exclusion from peace processes and peacebuilding-related activity as documented in the recent high-level review. These tensions are, in fact, irresolvable: those people that identify – or that are identified – as women, and the roles that they play, will continue to vary enormously, such that life experience continually confounds our theorisations and vice versa. Women are both the 'victims of violence' referenced in the title of this article, and the 'agents of change'. What is interesting to me is how the subject of 'women' is deployed in peacebuilding discourse, to create certain 'peacebuilding realities' that may – or may not – be related to the exclusions in practice noted above. It is important to understand how actors and institutions attach meaning to subjects, because through examining the construction of meaning, we examine the production of possibility: once a particular meaning is attached to 'women', for example, such as 'agent of change' or 'helpless victim', certain policy initiatives become 'thinkable', even necessary, while others are excluded.

This matters not only for women in peacebuilding but for peacebuilding more broadly: 'women's national, regional, and international involvement fundamentally shapes how peacebuilding projects and processes develop'.[20] In short, the active participation of women in peacebuilding changes the meaning of peacebuilding itself: different activities are recognised as part of peacebuilding practice, different power dynamics in society are laid bare and can be examined (even changed), and the relationship between peace and security is theorised differently. In this article, I show how the meanings attached to women, and forms of engagement with elements of the Women, Peace and Security agenda, are shaping peacebuilding at the United Nations.

Gendering UN peacebuilding: learning from his-story

The United Nations Peacebuilding Commission (UN PBC) is the advisory body that oversees peacebuilding strategies and operations under the auspices of the UN. Through the simultaneous adoption of resolutions in the UN General Assembly (60/180) and the UN Security Council (UNSCR 1645) in December 2005, this body was established to develop outlines of best practice in post-conflict reconstruction, and to secure the political and material resources necessary to assist states in transition from conflict to peace. The foundational resolution recognised that there was a 'need for a coordinated, coherent and integrated approach to post-conflict peacebuilding and reconciliation' and that this could be achieved by the creation of a 'dedicated institutional mechanism' which would be able to assist post-conflict countries in moving 'towards recovery, reintegration and reconstruction' while 'laying the foundation for sustainable development'.[21]

---

[19]Coomaraswamy et al., *Preventing Conflict*, 40.
[20]Cheryl de la Rey and Susan McKay, 'Peacebuilding as a Gendered Process', *Journal of Social Issues* 62, no. 1: 141–53, 150.
[21]United Nation Security Council, 'Resolution 1645', S/RES/1645, Preamble.

In this section, I analyse the documents gathered from the digital archive of the Commission, specifically the historical documents, statements from the Chair, and documentation from the Working Group on Lessons Learned, alongside the interview data produced during fieldwork, and argue that the Commission has not thus far achieved this coherence and integration. That should not be taken to mean, however, that the UN PBC is 'gender blind'; this is far from the case, as shown below.

The subject of women in peacebuilding discourse

The Chair of the UN Peacebuilding Commission rotates annually among the 31 members of the Organisational Committee. By convention, the Chair has made a statement to the Commission on the occasion of his election to the post and upon his departure (as mentioned, the Chair thus far has always been male). It was 2010 before a Chairperson mentioned women in an incoming or outgoing statement: 'we have to reinvigorate the vision behind the PBC. We have to follow up on the report *Peacebuilding in the Aftermath of Conflict*, and on Security Council Resolution 1889 – Women in Peacebuilding'.[22] It is notable that the statement regarding the Secretary-General's reports on 'Peacebuilding in the Immediate Aftermath of Conflict' and 'Women's Participation in Peacebuilding' made to the Security Council in 2011 on behalf of the Commission does not actually mention women's participation at all.[23]

A similar discursive dynamic is evident in the documentation from the Working Group on Lessons Learned (WGLL). The WGLL enables the Peacebuilding Commission to benefit from the expertise and experience of other actors by bringing together small groups of experts around a particular issue or in relation to a particular country context. The Chair of the Working Group usually provides 'Summary Notes' to the Commission outlining the discussion that took place when the key actors were convened. The first WGLL meetings were held in 2007, and included meetings on the country-specific contexts of Sierra Leone and Afghanistan, and the broader technical and conceptual issues of regional approaches to peacebuilding, the development of strategic frameworks, fiscal capacities in post-conflict environments and local governance in post-war contexts. Only the last of these mentions women at all, and none of the early WGLL documentation (up to and including documentation from 2007) refers to the Women, Peace and Security agenda or WPS principles.

The Chair's Summary Notes on local governance in post-war contexts is the only WGLL document from 2007 to mention women, perhaps reflecting the tendency among elite actors to associate women with informal political spaces.[24] This association denies much of the political work done by women both during 'peace time' and 'post-conflict'. As Aili Marie Tripp[25] has noted, the judgement about what constitutes political activity is itself a

---

[22]Peter Wittig, 'Statement by the Permanent Representative of Germany to the United Nations, H.E. Dr. Peter Wittig, on the occasion of his election as Chairman of the United Nations Peacebuilding Commission', 2010, http://www.un.org/en/peacebuilding/statements/pbc_chair/wahl_pbc_final_e_version.pdf (accessed January 5, 2106).

[23]Sylvie Lucas, 'Statement on Behalf of the PBC Chairperson at the Security Council meeting on Post-conflict Peacebuilding', United Nations, 2011, http://www.un.org/en/peacebuilding/pdf/sc_briefing-pbc_statement.pdf (accessed January 5, 2016).

[24]Often framed as 'local' and assumed to be 'apolitical' spaces, see Laura J. Shepherd, 'Constructing Civil Society: Gender, Power and Legitimacy in UN Peacebuilding Discourse', *European Journal of International Relations*, forthcoming; see also the classic essay on this topic, Sue Brownill and Susan Halford, 'Understanding Women's Involvement in Local Politics: How Useful is a Formal/Informal Dichotomy?' *Political Geography Quarterly* 9, no. 4 (1990): 396–414.

[25]Aili Marie Tripp, *Women & Politics in Uganda* (Madison, WS: University of Wisconsin Press, 2000), xvii.

political activity and one from which women are frequently excluded. The fact that women only feature as subjects in the context of a discussion about local governance in these early WGLL documents suggests that the Commission perpetuates the logic of political participation that associates women with local/civil politics rather than elite/formal government. That said, the document explicitly argues against this construction, proposing a model of government that 'involv[es] and empower[s] local people, including women and the poor'.[26] It would perhaps be churlish to object to women being singled out as a specific group in need of empowerment, along with the faceless, amorphous 'poor'. This clearly derives from the Background Note informing the discussion,[27] in which women (alone, p.4, and with children, p.3) feature as a simply part of the impoverished population: the 'voices' and 'concerns' of the poor 'especially women and children'[28] must be taken into account.

Women as victims or agents of change

The 2013 statement by the Chair at the conclusion of the 6th session was the first Chairperson's report to mention women *as* women (rather than as part of the title of the Secretary-General's report), in context of affirming Bangladesh's commitment to the goals and aspirations of the PBC:

> When Bangladesh achieved its independence through a devastating war in 1971 in which 3 million were killed, 10 million had to take shelter as refugees in neighbouring India including me, 30 million were displaced from their homes and nearly 250,000 of its young girls and women were dishonoured or raped.[29]

This account focuses on the vulnerability of women and depicts them as victims of violence rather than agents, a tension that emerged clearly in the interviews I conducted:

> there are two schools of thought, whether women need to be approached as victims of the fight or they are agents of change. And of course we are really moving towards both but more and more emphasis is now being put on the empowerment side meaning that they are the agents of change in society.[30]

This suggests a discursive shift that has found traction in peacebuilding discourse more broadly.

In the summary notes of the 2008 WGLL discussion on 'key insights, principles, good practices and emerging lessons', presented as a *Synthesis Report*,[31] the primary textual articulation is of women as agents of change:

> The founding resolutions [of the UN PBC] affirmed … the contribution of civil society and non-governmental organizations, including women's organizations, to peacebuilding efforts

---

[26]United Nations Peacebuilding Commission Working Group on Lessons Learned (UN PBC WGLL), 'Implementing Local Governance and Decentralisation Efforts: Chair's Summary', United Nations, 2007, http://www.un.org/en/peacebuilding/pdf/doc_wgll/decentralization_governance/wgll_chair_summary_13_12_07.pdf (accessed January 21, 2015): para. 2a.

[27]United Nations Peacebuilding Commission Working Group on Lessons Learned (UN PBC WGLL), 'Background Note: Local Governance and Decentralization in Post-war Contexts', United Nations, 2007, http://www.un.org/en/peacebuilding/pdf/doc_wgll/decentralization_governance/wgll_background_note_13_12_07.pdf (accessed January 21, 2015).

[28]UN PBC WGLL, 'Background Note: Local Governance and Decentralization', 3.

[29]Abdulkalam Abdul Momen, 'Statement of the Outcoming PBC Chair to the Formal OC', United Nations, 2013, http://www.un.org/en/peacebuilding/pdf/PBC%20Chair-Bangladesh-28Jan13-As%20delivered.pdf (accessed January 5, 2016).

[30]Interview 2, New York City, 2013.

[31]United Nations Peacebuilding Commission Working Group on Lessons Learned (UN PBC WGLL), 'Synthesis Report and Summary of Discussions: Key Insights, Principles, Good Practices and Emerging Lessons in Peacebuilding', United Nations, 2008, http://www.un.org/en/peacebuilding/pdf/doc_wgll/key_insights/synthesis_report_12_june08_conclusions.pdf (accessed January 22, 2015).

BUILDING PEACE

... [and] the important role of women in the prevention and resolution of conflicts and in peacebuilding.[32]

This stands in marked contrast to the other WGLL documents produced in 2008. The equal participation of women is framed as a necessary condition for the establishment of just and stable post-conflict societies[33] and women are framed as agents *first*: 'Women's agency ... must be acknowledged alongside their needs as victims.'[34] Violence is still represented as something that happens to women, however, and there is no acknowledgement in the text that women play multiple roles during conflict and post-conflict reconstruction including roles that involve perpetrating violence against men, other women and children.[35] An explicit link is drawn between the political participation of women and the prevention of sexualised and gender-based violence (SGBV), such that SGBV will 'never be properly addressed until there are sufficiently high numbers of women in decision-making positions at the peace table and in post-conflict national and local governments'.[36] This is a radical position for a UN entity to take; it recognises that women have the capacity to be agents of change in their societies and depicts them not as passive victims in need of protection but as political actors capable of enacting positive steps to, among other things, eliminate SGBV.[37]

The 'economic empowerment' of women

A particularly interesting contemporary element of UN peacebuilding discourse is the nature of the agency ascribed to women. Women have begun to be constructed as economic actors, such that a focus on women has seemingly become linked to economic empowerment: an example of this is the High-level Ministerial Meeting of the Peacebuilding Commission organised by representatives of Croatia in September 2013 on theme of 'Women's economic empowerment for peacebuilding'.

> The consensus Declaration emanating from this meeting did not only reaffirm our political commitment to support the economic empowerment of women for peacebuilding, it also showed the potentials of the PBC ... as a political and broad-based Member State platform.[38]

This is particularly interesting when cross-referenced with some interview data from a field visit in 2014, where the research participant comments that

> the declaration that came out of the Peacebuilding Commission's event ... was carefully negotiated word for word. This is the document that describes where the consensus is. This is the parameters of the consensual issues. The way there are described word for word because there were other words that were dropped because they do not reflect the consensus.[39]

This focus on women's economic empowerment is seen to be 'safer', politically, than a direct focus on women's political participation: this is a kind of 'stealth' approach to upholding

---

[32]UN PBC WGLL, 'Synthesis Report', 3.
[33]UN PBC WGLL, 'Synthesis Report', 10.
[34]Ibid.
[35]Moser and Clark, eds., *Victims, Perpetrators or Actors?* Laura Sjoberg and Caron E. Gentry, *Mothers, Monsters, Whores: Women's Violence in Global Politics* (London: Zed Books, 2007); Linda Åhäll and Laura J. Shepherd, eds., *Gender, Agency and Political Violence* (Basingstoke: Palgrave Macmillan, 2012).
[36]UN PBC WGLL, 'Synthesis Report and Summary of Discussions', 10.
[37]This construction can, of course, be interpreted as an implication that the elimination of SGBV becomes yet more 'women's work' in the conflict or post-conflict environment; such a concern speaks directly to the construction of women peacemakers as 'superheroines' posited by Cohn, Kinsella and Gibbings, above at Note 12.
[38]Vladimir Drobnjak, 'Statement of the Outgoing PBC Chair to the Formal OC', United Nations, 2014, http://www.un.org/en/peacebuilding/pdf/Statement-PBC%20Chair-handover-29Jan14.pdf (accessed January 5, 2016).
[39]Interview 4, New York City, 2014.

WPS principles, given what is noted above about the increase in social and political capital – and enhanced capacity to participate in formal politics – that women enjoy when they are able to engage in economic activity.[40] One research participant was very clear about the nature of this approach:

> the socio-economic side of the gender programming is something that everybody can agree to. Less so on the political and security side in terms of women mediators or the inclusion of women during the peace processes … an issue like women's participation in peacebuilding can actually degenerate into a very divisive discussion.[41]

The Chair of the Commission continued to emphasis women's participation in 2014, again linking participation to economics, noting 'the potential contribution of women's organizations in strengthening the economic role of women'.[42] Women are constructed here as active *economic* subjects, which in the discourse of the PBC appears to construct them as agential *political* subjects as well. In terms of the dynamics of neoliberal late modernity, this is particularly interesting. In order to participate politically, one must participate economically: to be a viable economic subject is to become a viable political subject. 'When women are economically empowered and earn their own money there is a sense of higher status in the community that really also has positive effects on politics participation'.[43] In the same speech quoted above, the Chair went on to reiterate that '[t]he transformative potential of greater women's participation in the economic and political spheres can bring an invaluable contribution to building more peaceful, democratic and prosperous societies'.[44] This repetition forges a strong link between the 'economic and political spheres', with the expectation on women that meaningful participation in one space will lead to meaningful participation in the other.

Gender mainstreaming or 'a gender perspective'

In this section I examine the overarching logics of gender in UN peacebuilding discourse, investigating how UN peacebuilding discourse represents gender, rather than women. In his outgoing statement in 2013, the Chair identified 'economic revitalization, gender mainstreaming, education and job creation as a central theme for 2013'.[45] 'Gender mainstreaming' is used interchangeably with the construction of gender as a 'dimension' of other themes by the Chair in 2014:

> Recognizing the important contribution of women to peacebuilding efforts, the Commission approached its thematic focus on economic revitalization and national reconciliation during the reporting period by examining the gender dimensions of both themes. A partnership with UN Women has enabled the Commission to explore the transformative role of women in post-conflict societies. … A meeting of the Working Group on Lessons Learning in December 2013 also reaffirmed the importance of gender mainstreaming in planning, priority setting, design and delivery of national reconciliation processes.[46]

---

[40]Interview 1, New York City, 2014.

[41]See note 30 above.

[42]Ibid.

[43]See note 40 above.

[44]de Aguiar Patriota, 'Statement by the Chair of the Peacebuilding Commission'.

[45]Momen, 'Statement of the Outcoming PBC Chair'.

[46]Vladimir Drobnjak, 'Presentation to the General Assembly of the Report of the Peacebuilding Commission on its Seventh Session', United Nations, 2014, http://www.un.org/en/peacebuilding/pdf/Draft%20Statement-PBC%20report%20on7th%20session-GA-DRAFT-26MAR14.pdf (accessed January 5, 2016); the same language is used in a presentation to the UN Security Council on Post-Conflict Peacebuilding on 15 July 2014.

As well as an assumption that 'the gender dimension' applies to women only, there appears to be institutional ambivalence about the concept of 'gender mainstreaming', which is in keeping with much of the scholarly literature on this topic.[47]

A key issue with gender mainstreaming as an approach is its lack of clarity, a fuzziness around what it would/should look like when gender has been 'mainstreamed' through a particular programme or policy process. A further concern is the concomitant lack of accountability: if paying attention to gender is everyone's responsibility, it is too easy for it to become no one's responsibility. This perhaps accounts for the reframing of the issue by research participants:

> we have a very clear program of work around the seven-point action plan of the Secretary-General's report on women's participation in peacebuilding of 2010. So that's what really drives us. I mean, you can call it gender mainstreaming but it also actually is not.[48]

It is noteworthy that it is the Secretary-General's report that 'drives' gender-responsive peacebuilding at the UN rather than the WPS resolutions.

The Working Group on Lessons Learned was at its most active in 2008, when the Group convened eight meetings on different themes: gender and peacebuilding; transitional justice; internal displacement; environmental conservation; key insights and best practice in peacebuilding; comparative lessons from the UN Rule of Law assistance; DDR (disarmament, demobilisation and reintegration) approaches; and developing national capacities after conflict. It is noteworthy that the majority of the WGLL documents from this period discuss women, with the surprising exceptions of the documentation on the DDR meeting and the documentation on the meeting about environmental challenges. It is less surprising, as discussed above, that women tend to be depicted in terms of their 'needs'[49] and their specific 'vulnerability'.[50] That said, the *Synthesis Report*[51] mentioned above, lists the inclusion of a 'gender perspective' as one of the common principles that should guide all peacebuilding-related activity undertaken under the auspices of the Commission.[52] This is a significant document in the evolution of the UN PBC, as it not only consolidates the role and function of the Commission but also reaffirms the importance of the Working Group as 'an ad hoc body open to all member states, institutional donors and representatives of civil society'[53] as well as setting the future agenda for the Working Group.[54] It is important, in terms of institutional visibility, that gender is identified as an issue that cuts across all dimensions of peacebuilding work.[55] The *Synthesis Report* also remind the Commission of

---

[47]Emilie Hafner-Burton and Mark A. Pollack, 'Mainstreaming Gender in Global Governance', *European Journal of International Relations* 8, no. 3 (2002): 339–73; Mary Daly, 'Gender Mainstreaming in Theory and in Practice', *Social Politics: International Studies in Gender, State and Society* 12, no. 3 (2005): 433–50; Caroline Moser and Annalise Moser, 'Gender Mainstreaming Since Beijing: A Review of Success and Limitations in International Institutions', *Gender and Development* 13, no. 2 (2005): 11–22.

[48]Interview 3, New York City, 2014.

[49]United Nations Peacebuilding Commission Working Group on Lessons Learned (UN PBC WGLL), 'Justice in Times of Transition: Chair's Summary', United Nations, 2008, http://www.un.org/en/peacebuilding/pdf/doc_wgll/justice_times_transition/26_02_2008_chair_summary.pdf (accessed January 21, 2015), para. 5.

[50]United Nations Peacebuilding Commission Working Group on Lessons Learned (UN PBC WGLL), 'Durable Solutions for Internally Displaced Persons: An Essential Dimension of Peacebuilding', United Nations, 2008, http://www.un.org/en/peacebuilding/pdf/doc_wgll/comparative_lessons_internal_displacement/13_03_2008_background_note.pdf (accessed January 21, 2015), 5.

[51]See note 31 above.

[52]UN PBC WGLL, 'Synthesis Report', 1.

[53]UN PBC WGLL, 'Synthesis Report', 2.

[54]UN PBC WGLL, 'Synthesis Report', 15–16.

[55]UN PBC WGLL, 'Synthesis Report', 9.

the mandate in the foundational resolution of the UN PBC to mainstream gender in all of its work, [56] and includes a reference to UNSCR 1325 as a 'normative framework' that enjoys 'widespread acceptance'.[57] The summary of the 2008 'lesson learned' about the inclusion of 'a gender perspective' is as follows:

> men and women are affected differently by conflict. Any peacebuilding strategy should address these differences, especially to ensure the end of impunity for gender-based violence, while contributing to gender equality and supporting women's full participation in and ownership of peacebuilding and recovery.

It is clear that the principles enshrined in the resolution are part of the knowledge base of the Peacebuilding Commission (or were in June 2008).

In 2009, the recognition that gender 'cut[s] across various dimensions' of peacebuilding[58] is diluted; we find only a vague reference to 'the role of women'[59] in the 2009 'taking stock' document produced at the end of the year (an updated version of the 2008 'key insights' document).[60] The importance of gender-responsive peacebuilding and/or the capacities of women to contribute to building more stable peace are highlighted in papers on youth employment (2010),[61] security sector reform (2011),[62] resource mobilisation (2012),[63] and the transition of UN missions (2014).[64] Engagement is frequently quite shallow, however; the youth employment paper, for example, mentions only that 'a clear perspective on how the gender dimension can be incorporated in economic activities' has yet to be developed.[65] Representing 'the gender dimension' as a singular, monolithic *thing* that needs to be 'incorporated' suggests a lack of nuance in understanding the many and various ways in which formal and informal economies are gendered.[66] Similarly, the most prominent articulation of women in the 2012 resource mobilisation document is in the statement from the Permanent Representative of Guinea who challenged the focus of the Commission's activities, arguing that security-led peacebuilding activity is 'not matched by attention to the other two peacebuilding priorities, namely youth and women empowerment and national reconciliation, which remain largely unaddressed'.[67]

---

[56]See note 33 above.

[57]UN PBC WGLL, 'Synthesis Report', 4.

[58]UN PBC WGLL, 'Synthesis Report and Summary of Discussions', 9.

[59]United Nations Peacebuilding Commission Working Group on Lessons Learned (UN PBC WGLL), 'The PBC Working Group on Lessons Learned: Taking Stock and Looking Forward – Chair's Summary', United Nations, 2009, http://www.un.org/en/peacebuilding/pdf/doc_wgll/wgll_wrap_up_chair_summary.pdf (accessed January 22, 2015).

[60]UN PBC WGLL, 'Synthesis Report and Summary of Discussions'.

[61]United Nations Peacebuilding Commission Working Group on Lessons Learned (UN PBC WGLL), 'Youth Employment in Peacebuilding Chairperson's Summary', United Nations, 2010, http://www.un.org/en/peacebuilding/pdf/doc_wgll/wgll_youth_employment_chairs_summary_14_July_2010.pdf (accessed January 22, 2015).

[62]United Nations Peacebuilding Commission Working Group on Lessons Learned (UN PBC WGLL), 'Security Sector Reform and Rule of Law for Peacebuilding: Chairperson's Summary', United Nations, 2011, http://www.un.org/en/peacebuilding/pdf/doc_wgll/Draft%20WGLL%20Chair's%20Summary-SSR&RoL-Final.pdf (accessed January 22, 2015).

[63]United Nations Peacebuilding Commission Working Group on Lessons Learned (UN PBC WGLL), 'Resource Mobilization and Mapping of Relevant Actors: Chairperson's Summary', United Nations, 2012, http://www.un.org/en/peacebuilding/wgll/Draft%20WGLL%20Chair's%20Summary-Resource%20Mob%20%20Mapping_Final%20to%20disseminate.pdf (accessed January 22, 2015).

[64]United Nations Peacebuilding Commission Working Group on Lessons Learned (UN PBC WGLL), 'Final Report of the PBC Working Group on Lessons Learned: Transition of UN Missions: What Role for the PBC?' United Nations, 2014, http://www.un.org/en/peacebuilding/wgll/141212%20WGLL%20Final%20Report.pdf (accessed January 22, 2015).

[65]UN PBC WGLL, 'Youth Employment in Peacebuilding', 4.

[66]See V. Spike Peterson, *A Critical Rewriting of Global Political Economy: Integrating Reproductive, Productive and Virtual Economies* (London: Routledge, 2003); and Penny Griffin, *Gendering the World Bank: Neoliberalism and the Gendered Foundations of Global Governance* (Basingstoke: Palgrave Macmillan, 2009).

[67]UN PBC WGLL, 'Resource Mobilization and Mapping of Relevant Actors', 2.

The most recent documentation outlining 'lessons learned' by the Peacebuilding Commission about gender-responsive peacebuilding relate to processes of national reconciliation.[68] The discussion on this topic identifies the development of recommendations for peacebuilding practice as a key priority, as this will 'strengthen the implementation of the Secretary-General's Seven Point Action Plan'.[69] The Chair's summary notes are particularly significant, as, for the first time in this suite of documents, explicit mention is made of the Women, Peace and Security resolutions. The rationale provided for organising a meeting on the theme of gender and national reconciliation is the adoption of UN Security Council Resolution 2122 in October 2013, which 'places the focus on women's leadership and participation in conflict prevention, resolution, and peacebuilding'.[70] While this framing of the significance of UNSCR 2122 ignores the fact that the Commission should have been upholding WPS principles since its inception, in accordance with the first operative paragraph of UNSCR 1325, it is nonetheless encouraging to see the explicit articulation of the significance of one of the most recent WPS resolution for the work of the UN PBC.

One of the research participants I spoke with described the UN approach to gender-responsive peacebuilding as operating within a 'normative framework', noting the existence of 'some operational tools including the seven-point action plan'[71] but not commenting at all on the Women, Peace and Security agenda. There is an interesting tendency to describe the WPS agenda as a 'normative' agenda, and to engage with questions of women's participation as normative questions. This is in part due to a perceived lack of hard data on the difference that it makes to have women leading peace processes and peacebuilding-related activities:

> there is a very strong democratic human rights argument for the need to have women at the table ... but I think there is very little research on that to really make that point. Does it make a different if you have 50 per cent of the signatories as women on the peace agreement as compared to none for peaceful societies in the future?[72]

Further, given that this interview was conducted prior to the passage of recent WPS resolutions, including UNSCR 2122 which has exceptionally strong accountability mechanisms for a WPS resolution,[73] it will be interesting to see whether peacebuilding discourse changes again in the future to reflect better integration with the WPS agenda.

The limited direct engagement with the WPS agenda in both the document corpus and the interview data should not, however, be interpreted to mean that UN peacebuilding activity does not take account of the gendered power dynamics that create and are formed in all kinds of peace and security governance. One of the research participants I spoke with had a very clear vision of what 'good' gender-responsive peacebuilding should look like:

> ... a real good gender responsive project doesn't have to be, in my eyes, a project that has for a primary objective women's empowerment. It can be a digging a well project, but that has consulted women on where the well should be, on what's the right hand pump to use and what are the safety measures that the project should support to ensure that they can go there without being raped et cetera ... To me, that's a great gender project, and that's a great gender responsive

---

[68]United Nations Peacebuilding Commission Working Group on Lessons Learned (UN PBC WGLL), 'Enhancing Gender-responsive National Reconciliation Processes', Chair's Summary, United Nations, 2013, http://www.un.org/en/peacebuilding/wgll/WGLL%20CHAIR%20SUMMARY_Gender%20Response%20National%20Reconciliation%20Processes_FINAL_29%2012%2013%20_clean_.pdf, (accessed January 22, 2015).
[69]Ibid., 1.
[70]Ibid.
[71]Interview 5, New York City, 2013.
[72]See note 48 above.
[73]See Shepherd, 'Advancing the Women, Peace and Security Agenda'.

project, even though the objective is not to empower women, or in that case challenge gender norms because we're not saying women shouldn't go to the wells. We're saying let's make sure they can go there safely and actually use them.[74]

There is a certain pragmatism about this approach, one that separates out different elements of women's empowerment such that formal political activity is assumed to be separate from their ability to go about their daily lives securely. I would venture that these are not such separate issues, and that this 'gender-responsive project' contributes directly to women's empowerment.

Finally, the Commission faces a good deal of resistance from member states at the UN, felt particularly keenly given its status as an advisory body. Different state representatives support and challenge different elements of the WPS agenda, both in discussions at the Commission and at the UN Security Council:

> there are champions of the gender dimension of peacebuilding and the question of women's participation in peacebuilding … Its definitely there are a lot of champions, still, from the Western side of the membership [of the Security Council] but also it is getting there where some of the other major countries from the South [are] … highlighting it over and over again in terms of the need to involve women in the early stages.[75]

Implicitly, some of the 'Western side' and some of the 'major countries from the South' do not support the need to involve women in peacebuilding-related activity. The different levels of state support for various WPS principles were also highlighted in another interview:

> the agenda that was put at 2010 through the seven-point action plan … the majority of those seven points are problematic for some member states. Especially those that have to do with the competence in parliament, participation in mediation efforts, the certain amount of women on the table of a negotiation of a peace agreement.[76]

Again, we can see that the policy architecture that is the cause of the contestation is the Secretary-General's seven-point action plan, rather than the WPS agenda. This representation renders invisible more than a decade of WPS activity that made the Secretary-General's report both possible and necessary, even as it upholds the principles that structure the WPS agenda.

Conclusion: peacebuilding and the 'Women, Peace and Security' agenda

Peacebuilding-related activities under the auspices of the United Nations are not limited to those undertaken by the UN Peacebuilding Commission, although this research focusses primarily on UN PBC documentation.[77] That said, '[t]he Peacebuilding Commission has the distinction of being the first United Nations body to have the gender dimension explicitly built into its founding Resolutions'.[78] Given that the Women, Peace and Security agenda is the primary policy architecture through which gender issues relevant to, and the gendered political dynamics of, peace and conflict are addressed within the United Nations system, it is reasonable to expect coherence and integration of WPS principles and objectives in the discourse of the UN PBC. The activities of the Commission have been reviewed twice,

---

[74]See note 71 above.
[75]See note 30 above.
[76]See note 39 above.
[77]Research participants were employed in offices across the UN system and in civil society organisations based in New York.
[78]United Nations General Assembly/United Nations Security Council, 'Review of the United Nations peacebuilding architecture', A/64/868–S/2010/393, 21 July 2010, para. 29.

in 2010 and 2015, with the evaluation of gender-responsive peacebuilding-related activities and efforts made to increase women's participation in peace and security governance included in both reviews. The recommendations of the most recent review, which engages much more comprehensively with the gendered dynamics of peacebuilding than the 2010 review, reference *inter alia* the need ensure that proposed related UN Security Council and UN General Assembly resolutions reference existing resolutions that recognise 'the importance of gendered approaches to protection, prevention and participation for successful peacebuilding'.[79]

In this article, I have briefly explained the tension in representational practice that structures much academic and policy engagement with women in peacebuilding: the tension between representing women as 'victims of violence' or as 'agents of change'. In my analysis of UN peacebuilding discourse, I found a surprising lack of direct integration of the WPS agenda. Historically, the WPS agenda does not feature prominently in the discursive artefacts of the UN Peacebuilding Commission, and even in contemporary spoken discourse on peacebuilding, references to the WPS agenda are rare. The 'whole-of-UN' approach demanded in UNSCR 2122 may well bring about a discursive shift at the Commission, but in the meantime WPS principles are driven by association with the UN Secretary-General's report on women's participation in peacebuilding and the related seven-point action plan. This is potentially problematic as it locates responsibility – and authority – in the office of the Secretary-General, rendering invisible the decades of women's civil society organisation that both facilitated the development of the WPS agenda and ensures its perpetuation.

Women's participation in peacebuilding seems to be strongly tied to their subjectivity as economic agents. The devotion of a High-Level Ministerial Meeting of the Commission to the issue of women's economic empowerment for peacebuilding – one of only two meetings at this level since the inception of the Commission – is illustrative of the significance of this configuration of subjectivity. The association between women and economic empowerment not only suggests that the economic realm is a further space in which we are 'expecting more of women',[80] as cautioned by Cohn, Kinsella and Gibbings, but also functions to depoliticise economic activity. This happens through the implication that empowering women economically is a straightforward, technical exercise, unlike empowering them politically, which is implicitly complicated by extant configurations of gendered power. This is clearly not the case, as the decades of feminist scholarship on the gendered international *politics* of the economy referenced above demonstrates. The neoliberal politics of the kinds of microbusiness initiatives touted as optimal modes of engagement for women in emergent economies should also be noted here.[81]

Peacebuilding discourse at the UN repeatedly references women as agents of change. There is a strong emphasis on women's agency in the peacebuilding discourse I examine above, and repeated articulations of 'women's participation in peacebuilding' in both spoken discourse and documents. The function of having this phrase repeated so often in written texts and spoken discourse forges a strong association between women and peacebuilding

---

[79]United Nations General Assembly/United Nations Security Council, 'Challenge of Sustaining Peace: Report of the Advisory Group of Experts on the Review of the Peacebuilding Architecture', A/69/968–S/2015/490, 30 June 2015, para. 190.

[80]Cohn, Kinsella and Gibbings, 'Women, Peace and Security: Resolution 1325', 136.

[81]See, for example, Sylvia Chant, 'Women, Girls and World Poverty: Empowerment, Equality or Essentialism?' *International Development Planning Review*, 38, no. 1 (2016): 1–24; Jason Hickel, 'The "Girl Effect": Liberalism, Empowerment and the Contradictions of Development', *Third World Quarterly*, 35, no. 8 (2014): 1355–73; Naila Kabeer, 'Is Microfinance a "Magic Bullet" for Women's Empowerment? Analysis of Findings from South Asia', *Economic and Political Weekly*, 44, no. 44–5 (2005): 4709–18.

practice, normalising women's participation and simultaneously emphasising its importance. While I would politically prefer to see an acknowledgement of the political and normative significance of the WPS agenda, the dominant discourse of peacebuilding at the UN is one in which women are envisioned as agents, not just victims, and gender-responsive peacebuilding involves everything from election politics to well digging. While gaps and challenges remain, the potentialities enabled by these discursive constructions move those women whose lives are shaped by the peacebuilding-related activities they undertake closer to meaningful participation and the recognition of multiplicity that they deserve.

Acknowledgements

This article is part of a larger project investigating logics of gender and space in UN peacebuilding activities. Funding for this research is provided by the Australian Research Council (DP130100707). Caitlin Hamilton provided invaluable research assistance and support in the preparation of this article. I would also like to thank the two reviewers, who provided comprehensive, constructive and expert feedback on every article in this Special Issue, including my own. Finally, I am grateful to the journal editors for encouraging me to put together this collection, and for their patience in its execution.

Disclosure statement

No potential conflict of interest was reported by the author.

Funding

This work was supported by the Australian Research Council [grant number DP130100707].

A seat at the table is not enough: understanding women's substantive representation in peace processes

Kara Ellerby

Department of Political Science and International Relations, Women and Gender Studies, University of Delaware, Newark, DE, USA

ABSTRACT

While the international community stresses the importance of including women at the peace table so peace processes will better represent their needs and interests, it is unclear what specifically this inclusion entails. Do women need to be negotiators, mediators? Do peace agreements adequately represent women's interests when women are included? This article engages UNSC Resolution 1325 on Women, Peace and Security as a framework through which to assess peace processes and agreements. A woman-focused examination of all civil war peace processes reveals that less than 10% meet women's inclusion as envisioned in UNSCR 1325. This article focuses on the three conditions accounting for women's substantive representation in peacebuilding. What emerges are three joint necessities: an explicit women's *agenda*; *access* to the peace process; and *advocacy* within the process. The final sections problematise how even in all of these positive cases women had to fight to participate.

In 2009, United Nations Secretary General Ban Ki-Moon, in a statement about United Nations Security Council Resolution 1325 on Women, Peace and Security (UNSCR 1325), said that the international community must prevent 'any exclusion of women in peace negotiations and mediation … Indeed, a growing body of evidence suggests that bringing women to the peace table improves the quality of agreements reached, and increases the chances of successful implementation'.[1] Women's inclusion in peacebuilding remains an issue of great significance and relevance, not least because peace processes remain overwhelmingly male-dominated and male-centred. One of the oft-cited statistics from UN Women highlights this reality: in a study of thirty-one processes between 1992 and 2010, only 2.5% of negotiators, 4% of signatories and 9% of delegations were women.[2]

As this article argues, however, these figures may represent an over-simplification of the complicated processes through which women (and men) can actively participate and

---

[1] United Nations Secretary General 'Secretary-General Says Security Council Resolution 1325 Was "Milestone" on Issue of Women's Role in Peace and Security,' press release, October 5, 2009.

[2] UN Women, 'Women's Participation in Peace Negotiations: Connections between Presence and Infl uence' (2012), http://www.unwomen.org/~/media/headquarters/attachments/sections/library/publications/2012/10/wpssource-book-03a-womenpeacenegotiations-en.pdf (accessed January 2, 2015).

shape peace. Women's participation as negotiators and mediators may not be enough to guarantee more woman-identified peacebuilding, of course. El Salvador, for example, is often considered a 'successful' peace process because both the government and rebels respected the ceasefire and disarmament was fairly successful.[3] If success is conceived of differently, however, and is related to the degree to which women and women's interests are included in the process, the evaluation of El Salvador is decidedly less positive. The Chapultepec Peace Agreement contains only one reference to women in a section on the National Public Security Academy: 'A publicity campaign to promote the recruitment of new personnel for the National Civil Police shall be designed and implemented as soon as possible. *Special consideration shall be given to the recruitment of women*' (1992). According to Clara Murguialday:

> Neither in words nor spirit is there any reference to women, despite the fact that they represent 52.9% of the Salvadoran population, 30% of the 13,600 FMLN combatants that were verified, and more than 60% of the civilian population that supported the guerillas during the armed conflict.[4]

Additionally, women *were* at the peace table as ranking members of the El Salvadoran rebel movement, FMLN (*Farabundo Martí Front for National Liberation*), but these women did not advocate for women's issues during negotiations. One commander told researchers she supported women's issues but did not bring them up and another female commander considered the women's movement 'extremist and radical' and not part of their overall movement.[5] So in this case, one woman appears to have felt silenced by the process while the other saw women's issues as competing with larger objectives. But the outcome is the same: these women did not advocate for women's peacebuilding and the peace agreement reflects these silences.

What emerges from such a case is an important puzzle: under what conditions does women's descriptive representation during peace processes result in their substantive representation in peace agreements? To put this slightly differently: when actual women participate in peace processes (descriptive representation), do peace agreements include more woman-centred provisions and better reflect women's interests (substantive representation)?[6] Importantly, the mere presence of some women alone does not appear to be enough when such women either feel silenced and/or do not identify as advocates for women's inclusion. To address this question, this article engages UNSCR 1325 as a framework to guide women's substantive representation in the study of peace processes and the agreements they produce.

The first part of the article outlines how UNSCR 1325 can be used as a framework to assess women's substantive representation in actual peace agreements. In applying this framework to civil wars over the last 25 years, one begins to see how infrequently women's interests are actually included. Based on these findings, I identify six cases in which women were substantively represented in peace agreements in a way that more broadly reflects

---

[3] Tommie Sue Montgomery, 'Getting to Peace in El Salvador: The Roles of the United Nations Secretariat and ONUSAL', *Journal of Interamerican Studies and World Affairs* 37, no. 4 (1995): 139–72.

[4] Cited from Karen Kampwirth, *Feminism and the Legacy of Revolution: Nicaragua, El Salvador, Chiapas* (Athens, OH: Ohio University Press, 2004), 81.

[5] Ilja A. Luciak, *After the Revolution: Gender and Democracy in El Salvador, Nicaragua, and Guatemala* (Baltimore: The Johns Hopkins Press, 2001), 39.

[6] This article defines descriptive representation as the presence of women's bodies in a given context and substantive representation as a set of outcomes (policy, discourses) reflecting women's ideas and interests, reflected through language mentioning women and/or gender.

the mandates of UNSCR 1325. Working backwards from brief studies of these cases, what emerges are three jointly necessary conditions for more woman-inclusive peace agreements: a women's *agenda*; women's *access* to the process; and *advocacy* from parties to the conflict. Ultimately, this article argues that women's descriptive representation does matter for women's substantive representation, although women's inclusion is more multifaceted than mere presence, requiring active participation by women as well as institutional support. In the final section, I show that all these cases share one other important attribute: the consistent resistance to women's participation more generally and the ways in which women have to insist and agitate to be considered stakeholders. This illustrates the continued pervasiveness of gendered binary logics of masculine–feminine and war-peace in peacebuilding.

Women in peace?

Peace studies as a discipline has a long history of engaging the complexities of ending hostilities and resolving conflict. This body of research generally focuses on governments, belligerents and mediators and their strategies for managing direct violence and addressing underlying causes of conflict. This rather narrow meaning for primary stakeholders and the central focus on how formal actors participle has resulted in a dearth of knowledge about women's participation and engagements with peace in mainstream peace studies.[7] Women's peace activities are often treated as secondary to formal peace processes, often under the guise of 'gender neutral' processes,[8] despite a prolific and practical body of research on women and what they do to promote peace.[9]

Resolving state-level conflict is of primary concern for many women for a number of reasons. The first, most obvious, reason is to end violence disrupting women's livelihoods and communities.[10] The second has to do with peace agreements as the beginning for a larger process of disruption of gender roles and women's subordination. Women in post-conflict may identify such moments of transition as 'windows of opportunity' from which to organise and demand change and there is quite a bit of evidence women do organise and create social and political change.[11] In this sense, peace and post-conflict opportunities for women are not about a return to the status quo,[12] but also a potential moment to disrupt gendered violence and exclusion moving forward.

Woman and gender-centred studies of conflict resolution often focus on how women work at local levels to bridge divides and encourage an end to fighting. For example, in Bougainville

---

[7]Georgina Waylen, 'A Seat at the Table- Is It Enough? Gender, Multiparty Negotiations, and Institutional Design in South Africa and Northern Ireland', *Politics & Gender* 10 (2014): 495–523.

[8]Sanam Anderlini, *Women Building Peace: What They Do, Why It Matters* (Boulder: Lynne Rienner, 2007); Elisabeth Porter, 'Women, Political Decision-Making, and Peace-Building', *Global Change, Peace & Security* 15, no. 3 (2003): 245; Dyan Mazurana and Susan McKay, *Women and Peacebuilding*. No. 8. International Centre for Human Rights and Democratic Development no. 8 (1999).

[9]Sanam Anderlini, *Women Building Peace*; Cynthia Cockburn, *From Where We Stand: War, Women's Activism and Feminist Analysis* (London: Zed Books, 2007); Sheila Meintjes, Meredeth Turshen, and Anu Pillay, *The Aftermath: Women in Post-Conflict Transformation* (London: Zed Books, 2001).

[10]Laura Sjoberg, *Gendering Global Conflict: Toward a Feminist Theory of War* (New York City: Columbia University Press, 2013).

[11]Julie Arostegui, 'Gender, Conflict, and Peace-Building: How Conflict Can Catalyse Positive Change for Women', *Gender & Development* 21, no. 3 (2013): 533–49; Judith El-Bushra, 'Feminism, Gender, and Women's Peace Activism', *Development and Change* 38, no. 1 (2007): 131.

[12]Kara Ellerby and Chiseche Mibenge, 'African Women as Peacebuilders: (Re)thinking Conflict Resolution', From the Symposium: 'New Directions in Gender and Politics Scholarship: Transforming the Study of African Politics'. African Politics Conference Group Newsletter 8, no. 2 (2012): 5–6.

(Papua New Guinea), women asked young soldiers to return home, organised demonstrations and meetings using churches.[13] In Uganda, women organised a peace caravan to call for a cessation to violence and promote their inclusion in the peace talks.[14] Mairead Corrigan and Betty Williams were awarded the 1977 Nobel Peace Prize for mobilising women in Northern Ireland demanding peace.[15] In Colombia, women were central in organising the Mandate for Peace, Life and Freedom Campaign, which included ten million signatures calling for a negotiated settlement to end the civil war.[16] And in Liberia, the now famous Liberian Women's Initiative demonstrated and held meetings across religious divides, prompting the award in 2011 of the Nobel Peace Prize to the founder, Lemah Gwboee. There are many stories of women's activism to end conflict, but such activism often appear to be practiced outside the narrow confines of formal peace processes. In other words, women's peace activism is not treated as a central component of formal ceasefires or comprehensive peace processes.

A previous UN study found there had never been a woman chief mediator (UNIFEM 2009), (though this has changed since the recent Philippines-Mindanao negotiations). In the peace processes in Tajikistan, Burundi, Kosovo and Northern Ireland, only one or two women were included as negotiators.[17] The general exclusion of women has a number of explanatory factors. The first reason is a 'selection effect' issue. Because women occupy fewer positions of traditional power within the 'peacemaker pipeline', in political parties, the state and powerful nonstate groups, there are just fewer women from which negotiators and mediators are selected.[18] The second major issue has to do with pervasive sexism, where beliefs about women and gender impact predilections to include women. Sanam Anderlini notes a belief among male policymakers that peace negotiations are not the right venue for discussing 'women's issues' and women do not represent the 'broad population' and that peace accords are 'gender neutral'.[19] Others have found that women are simply seen as unimportant.[20] What all of these reports signal is that women are generally not considered primary stakeholders in peace negotiations, and it is interesting to explore whether this translates to their exclusion from the formal outlines for future peacebuilding documented in peace agreements.

War and peace remain gendered concepts, in that they are often represented within a dichotomous frame in which war is masculine and peace, feminine. This construct is further embedded in beliefs about predilections for violence, where men are seen as violent and women as peaceful, despite such assumptions being thoroughly debunked.[21] These gendered ways of thinking persist and then inform beliefs and actions about who engages

---

[13]Pat Howley, *Breaking Spears and Mending Hearts: Peacemakers and Restorative Justice in Bougainville* (Sydney: Federation Press, 2002); Ruth Saovana-Spriggs, 'Bougainville Women's Role in Conflict Resolution in the Bougainville Peace Process', in *A kind of Mending: Restorative justice in the Pacific Islands*, ed. Sinclair Dinnen, Anita Jowitt, and Tess Newton Cain (Canberra: Pandanus Books, 2003), 195–214. Sources cited from Hilary Charlesworth, 'Are Women Peaceful? Reflections on the Role of Women in Peace-Building', *Feminist Legal Studies* 16, no. 3 (2008): 347–61.

[14]Aili Tripp et al., *African Women's Movements: Transforming Political Landscapes* (New York: Cambridge University Press, 2009).

[15]Anderlini, *Women Building Peace*, 257.

[16]Ibid.

[17]Porter, Elisabeth, *Peacebuilding: Women in International Perspective* (New York: Routledge, 2007).

[18]Anderlini, *Women Building Peace*, 58–61; Porter, *Women in Peacebuilding*.

[19]Anderlini, *Women Building Peace*, 61–2.

[20]Porter, *Women in Peacebuilding*.

[21]Charlesworth, 'Are Women Peaceful?'; Azza Karam, 'Women in War and Peace-Building: The Roads Traversed, The Challenges Ahead', *International Feminist Journal of Politics* 3, no. 1 (2000): 2; Helen Kinsella, *The Image before the Weapon: A Critical History of the Distinction between Combatant and Civilian* (New York: Cornell University Press, 2011); Laura Sjoberg and Caron E. Gentry, *Mothers, Monsters, Whores: Women's Violence in Global Politics* (New York: Zed Books, 2008); J. Ann Tickner, *Gendering World Politics: Issues and Approaches in the Post-Cold War Era* (Columbia: Columbia University Press, 2001).

in conflict and who has a legitimate stake in building peace. As Hilary Charlesworth (2008) has discussed, this idea of 'women as peaceable' is now found in international legal documents and is treated as an orthodoxy among even women scholars who focus on what women offer in terms of peace (women as more ethical, bridge-builders, transformative, and so on). Even those working to advocate for more women in peacebuilding can utilise the same problematic tropes in their efforts for change.

According to the logic of women-as-more-peaceful, one would perhaps expect women to be more active in formal peacebuilding activities – they are often described via their skills as mediators and educators in their own communities, but this is not how the (il)logic operates. Rather, it is the underlying belief about conflict and violence as a masculine domain, and thus the preserve of males, that informs beliefs and practices in two important ways. The first is that because of the belief that mainly men engage in (active) conflict, they are considered the central stakeholders in resolving it.[22] The second way this thinking operates is that because peace processes are (usually) treated as elite events in which parties to conflict and negotiators are considered the most relevant actors, women's participation in informal peacemaking and via civil society is considered secondary and often not at all relevant to formal peace negotiations and processes. In other words, women are not considered primary stakeholders in peace processes because gendered belief systems promote the idea only those deemed to have participated in active conflict (men) are equipped to actually create peace.

If women are not often included in formal peace negotiations, to what degree does this have an impact on outcomes? More specifically, does women's descriptive exclusion from peace processes result in their substantive exclusion from peace agreements? The next section engages UNSCR 1325 as a framework for women's inclusion in 'peace', which allows for a more critical interrogation of the degree to which women's security concerns and peacebuilding interests are and are not included in formal peace agreements. It is from there that we can begin to understand where peacebuilding for and by women has been successful and what may account for that in a world where women's exclusion remains the norm.

UNSCR 1325: a framework for women's substantive representation

Widely acknowledged for its continuing importance and agenda-setting power,[23] United Nations Security Council Resolution 1325 on Women, Peace and Security (2000) outlined how to better include women and address women's concerns in resolving conflict. UNSCR 1325 was passed after the activist efforts of civil society organisations and NGOs pushed for a global to need to recognise and challenge women's exclusion from peace processes.[24] While outlining its practical implementation and empirical effects has been challenging,[25]

---

[22] Judy El-Bushra, 'Feminism, Gender, and Women's'.

[23] Louise Olsson and Theodora-Ismene Gizelis, 'An Introduction to UNSCR 1325', *International Interactions* 39, no. 4 (2013): 425–34.

[24] Carol Cohn, 'Feminist Peacemaking: In Resolution 1325, the United Nations Requires the Inclusion of Women in All Peace Planning and Negotiation', *The Women's Review of Books* 21, no. 5 (February 2004): 8–9; Carol Cohn, 'Mainstreaming Gender in UN Security Policy: A Path to Political Transformation?' in *Global Governance* (London: Palgrave Macmillan, 2008), 185–206; Chantal de Jonge Oudraat, 'UNSCR 1325 – Conundrums and Opportunities', *International Interactions* 39, no. 4 (2013): 612–19.

[25] Sanam Anderlini, 'What The Women Say: Participation and UNSCR 1325', International Civil Society Action Network and MIT Center for International Studies (2010), http://web.mit.edu/cis/pdf/WomenReport_10_2010.pdf; Christina Binder, Karin Lukas, and Romana Schweiger, 'Empty Words or Real Achievement? The Impact of Security Council Resolution 1325 on Women in Armed Conflicts', *Radical History Review* 2008, no. 101 (2008): 22–41; Christine Chinkin and Hillary Charlesworth, 'Building Women into Peace: The International Legal Framework', *Third World Quarterly* 27, no. 5 (2006): 937–57; Olsson and Gizelis, 'An Introduction to UNSCR 1325'.

the overview presented below outlines the use of UNSCR 1325 as an empirical framework to assess documents and activities and how well they reflect the mandates within UNSCR 1325. This can be effective for assessing women's peacebuilding efforts and outcomes because it directly engages how women's participation in peacebuilding is outlined in a binding global document.

Since women's exclusion from peace processes is considered the most important barrier to representing their interests, woman-centred peacebuilding should reflect women's substantive representation, meaning that women's participation and interests are reflected in the agreement. In this capacity, I have derived from UNSCR 1325 four ways in which women should be included in peacebuilding that can ensure their substantive needs are represented and addressed: *representation, incorporation, protection and recognition.*[26] *Representation* focuses on including women as decision-makers and in leadership positions, not only in public office but also transitional commissions and temporary bodies of peacebuilding efforts. *Incorporation* focuses on how to include women in the day-to-day practices of peacebuilding. Women need to be included in the military and police and in generally male-dominated institutions, not just as leaders, but as rank-and-file personnel. *Protection* focuses on making sure women are included in legal codes, that their safety and security against gendered violence counts as criminal, and that women's rights are specifically protected under the law. Finally, *recognition* is the inclusion of women's interests or women as a specific group whose interests should be addressed in the construction and implementation of constitutions and new legal parameters as the country designs political infrastructure.

Having an empirical framework of substantive representation and inclusion rather than just counting the number of times women and/or gender is mentioned in agreements is important. If agreements only address one area of women's concerns, but not others, this can then be conceived of as limited substantive representation. For example, a peace agreement may call for quotas for women's representation in government offices and transitional committees but then neglect issues of policing and security or changes to constitutions. In this sense, by categorising different ways of including women, one can better assess the breadth to which such agreements articulate women's inclusion.

Using this framework, I undertook a textual analysis of all negotiated civil war peace processes and their agreements between 1991 and 2014. The data were collected from three data sets and databases for the agreements, including Uppsala Conflict Data Program's Peace Agreement Data-set,[27] the Transitional Justice Institute Peace Agreement Database[28] and UN Peacemaker[29] (2014). In total, there were 57 peace processes entailing a few hundred agreements. The unit of analysis is the peace process, meaning if the process included more than one agreement related to the same conflict, these were treated as part of the same unit. For example, Guatemala had eleven agreements that were considered part of one comprehensive peace agreement (CPA), so the eleven documents are considered part of one process.

---

[26]For further discussion of this measure see Kara Ellerby, '(En)gendered Security? The Complexities of Women's Inclusion in Peace Processes', *International Interactions* 39, no. 4 (2013): 435–60.

[27]Lotta Harbom, Stina Högbladh, and Peter Wallensteen. 'Armed Conflict and Peace Agreements', *Journal of Peace Research* 43, no. 5 (2006): 617–31; Stina Hogbladh, 'Peace Agreements 1975–2011 – Updating the UCDP Peace Agreement Data-set', Uppsala Conflict Data Program, 2012.

[28]Christine Bell and Catherine O'Rourke. 'Peace Agreement Database' (2010), http://www.transitionaljustice.ulster.ac.uk/tji_database.html.

[29]United Nations, *Peace Agreements Database Search* (2014), http://peacemaker.un.org/document-search (accessed December 1, 2014).

BUILDING PEACE

Table 1. Peace processes according to level of substantive representation.

	No substantive representation	1 Category of substantive representation	2 Categories of substantive representation	3 Categories of substantive representation	4 Categories of substantive representation
1990–1993	Cambodia Slovenia India (Tripur) India (Bodoland) Afghanistan	El Salvador Mali Mozambique Rwanda Somalia			
1994–1996	Georgia Croatia Niger	Bosnia-Serbia Philippines	Liberia (LURD)	Mexico	Guatemala
1997–1999	Bosnia (Croat) Moldova Tajikistan Guinea Bissau Congo Yugoslavia	Bangladesh Israel	UK		
2000–2002	Djibouti Macedonia Colombia	Sierra Leone Papua New Guinea Angola			Burundi
2003–2005	Comoros Senegal Indonesia	Sudan (CPA)	Liberia (NPF)		DRC
2006–2009	Central African Republic	Ivory Coast Somalia DRC (Kivu)	Kenya	Zimbabwe	Sudan (DPA) Uganda
2010–2014	Chad Myanmar	Central African Republic DRC (M23) Mali			Philippines (Bangsamoro)

Based on the textual analysis of all 54 negotiated peace processes between 1991 and 2014, only 65% include *any* reference to women and/or gender. This would indicate women's overall substantive representation in peace agreements remains quite low.[30] Among the 34 cases that actually do engage these four ways to substantively represent women, the degree varies significantly and most only address one or two forms, as indicated in Table 1. Only six peace processes addressed all four forms of women's substantive representation in their agreements. Put another way, only six peace processes recognised women's substantive representation within larger peacebuilding frameworks to the degree expected in UNSCR 1325. These are the peace processes in Guatemala, Burundi, the Democratic Republic of Congo, Sudan's Darfur Peace Process, Uganda and the Philippines-Mindanao. Many of these cases would not be considered traditionally successful by mainstream standards because they did not end conflict, but in terms of women's substantive representation, these are the most thorough of them all. So what made these cases more substantively inclusive of women?

Women's substantive peace

To begin making sense of why only six cases adequately include women's peacebuilding objectives and interests, as shown in the fifth column in Table 1 ('4 Categories of Substantive

---

[30]For more discussion of trends over time in these data, see Kara Ellerby, '(En)gendered Security? Gender Mainstreaming and Women's Inclusion in Peace Processes', in *A Systematic Understanding of Gender, Peace and Security: Implementing UNSCR 1325*, ed. Ismene Gizelis and Louise Olsson (New York: Routledge, 2015), 185–209.

Representation'), the rest of this article examines them in more detail. As mentioned above, the El Salvador case indicates that just having women 'at the table' may not be enough; women can be part of the process and yet be so marginalised in the process that they are silenced and effectively excluded. Further, women may not consider women's issues central to the overall objectives of their movement, or could perceive competition between women's issues and overall objectives. Previous case study work on Sudan's CPA and Darfur Peace Agreement[31] outlined three conditions for a more woman-inclusive peace agreement: women should have their own agenda; they should have some space to be included in the process; and they should have support to make their claims. I use these three jointly necessary conditions to analyse these six cases below and the degree to which women participate in these processes. My findings indicate these three conditions are jointly necessary for a woman-inclusive peace agreement as they are found in all six cases.[32]

The first factor in explaining women's inclusion is a women's *agenda*. A women's agenda is basically a set of articulated and (usually) written provisions and priorities proposed to relevant parties in negotiations. The goal of a women's agenda is to outline when and how women should be included in peacebuilding activities, from representation in government and transitional committees to demands for changes in laws.

The second factor is *access*, which is meant to capture the degree to which women are able to participate in the formal peace process. Access should be understood as a continuum of possible involvement ranging from no access at all, to indirect and direct access to the process. If women have any access, it may be easier for them to present their agenda and be heard, which is often contingent on the third factor: leadership *advocacy*.

Advocacy captures the degree to which leadership (defined here as main parties to the conflict and mediators/negotiators) involved in peace processes consider women's inclusion *part* of the security process. Some processes treat women's rights and security as complementary to or a priority within broader goals while other processes consider women's demands as competing or detracting from their objectives. This sort of mentality on the part of warring parties, negotiators, mediators and observers may shape the degree to which women's access and agendas are actually included.

While I present each factor separately, it is important to note these factors are jointly necessary for greater levels of women's inclusion in peacebuilding. This means they must all be present, as they all are of equal importance and interdependent for understanding women's substantive representation in peace agreements.[33]

Women with an agenda

Through a careful reading of the six cases, I have found they all had some explicit women's agenda. The idea is that when women make clear (especially in writing) their demands, these are more likely to be included in the actual agreements. In Guatemala, women created

---

[31] Kara Ellerby, 'The Tale of Two Sudans: Engendered Security and Peace Processes', *USIP Case Studies in Conflict Management and Peacebuilding Series* (Washington DC: United States Institute of Peace, 2012).

[32] Charles Ragin, 'Fuzzy Sets and Necessary Conditions', in *Fuzzy-Set Social Science* (Chicago: University of Chicago Press, 2000), 2–29. Necessary conditions are established by 'working backward from instance of the outcome'. In this case, the cases are 4-category levels of inclusion, or the highest levels of any actual peace processes according to the agreements produced. At this point, I cannot say make any claims about sufficiency without including more cases. The findings are a starting point for greater theory building and should be studied with caution against any sort of universalisation.

[33] The distinctions I make between these three conditions are in no way discrete. In this sense, the research below presents only my interpretation and categorisation of information and events.

written general demands regarding: development and repatriation and reintegration; criminalising sexual harassment and domestic violence; expansion of women's citizenship rights and political participation; protection for indigenous women and general indigenous rights; and increased access for women to credit, housing, land and education.[34] Provisions relating to all these topics are included in one or more of the actual peace agreements, indicating the clear success the Women's Sector had in making their voices heard as part of the peace process.

The same is true of Burundi's process where women, during their own conference (further discussed below), produced the 'Women's Proposals to Engender the Draft Arusha Peace and Reconciliation Agreement' outlining their own demands. These included a quota for all branches of government, a change to land and property rights, ending impunity for sexual violence and equal access to education.[35] Ultimately, twenty-three of their recommendations were included.[36]

In the case of Darfur's Peace Agreement, there were various women's groups working in Darfur who worked through UNIFEM to present an agenda to the African Union mediators, many parts of which were included in the final agreement. In the DRC, during the first preparatory meeting for the Inter-Congolese Dialogue (ICD), women produced an open letter demanding better representation during the ICD because their numbers were so low for the preparatory meeting.[37] After this, previously disparate women's groups and delegates to the process were brought together at a conference to produce a unified declaration and plan of action 'for all women at the ICD' which was submitted to the head negotiator and upon which women then participated in negotiations.[38]

In Uganda, women did not have a specific written or unified agenda as in the other cases, but they were 'informing both the government of Uganda and the LRA of the community's demands, needs and priorities on each of the agenda items of the peace negotiation process', including 'gendered exclusions'.[39] These priorities were based upon the Uganda Women's Coalition for Peace's work in communities speaking with women and documenting their demands.[40] While their efforts were not as clearly laid out as the other cases, women did have an agenda, though not explicitly written or organised as a cohesive set of priorities.

In the Philippines, where years of negotiations between the Government and the Moro Islamic Liberation Front (MILF) finally resulted in the Comprehensive Agreement on the Bangsamoro in March 2014, women also had an agenda. While the information on this case still remains sparse, according to *UN Women*, Muslim women's groups met with MILF representatives in 2011 and discussed 'provisions for women in draft peace agreements'.[41] This agenda was developed during the Mindanao Women Conference on Peace and Security, which prompted the selection of two women to MILF's 'peace panel'. The statement about

---

[34]Anna Lorena Carillo and Norma Stoltz Chinchilla, 'From Urban Elite to Peasant Organizing: Agendas, Accomplishments, and Challenges of Thirty-Plus Years of Guatemalan Feminism, 1975–2007', in *Women's Activisms in Latin America and the Caribbean*, eds. Elizabeth Maier and Nathalie Lebon (New Burnswick, NJ: Rutgers Press, 2010), 140–58.

[35]According to the All-Party Burundi Women's Peace Conference, cited from Tripp et al., *African Women's Movements*.

[36]Ibid.

[37]Shelly Whitman, 'Women and Peace-Building in the Democratic Republic of the Congo: An Assessment of the Their Role in the Inter-Congolese Dialogue', *African Journal on Conflict Resolution* 6, no. 1 (2007): 29–48.

[38]Tripp et al., *African Women's Movements*; Whitman, 'Women and Peace-Building'.

[39]Harriet Nabukeera-Musoke, 'Transitional Justice and Gender in Uganda: Making Peace, Failing Women During the Peace Negotiation Process', *African Journal on Conflict Resolution* 9, no. 2 (2009): 121–9.

[40]Ibid.

[41]UN Women, 'Conflict Prevention and Resolution', http://www.unwomen.org/en/what-we-do/peace-and-security/conflict-prevention-and-resolution (accessed February 3, 2016).

this conference indicates those women participating in this conference actively engaged UNSCR 1325 to make their case and advocate for formal participation in the formal cease-fire monitoring team, which included an all-women unit.[42] Their participation is reflected in their 'points of action' for beginning the talks in 2012, which included encouraging and supporting 'intra-dialogue from the ranks of the Moro political leaders, youth and women'.[43]

Based on these cases, we can identify a variety of ways in which women produce 'agendas'. In Guatemala, Burundi and Mindanao, women's demands were included in actual agreements. In the DRC, Darfur and Uganda, the agenda was less specific, not so much a written set of provisions but broader discourse calling for women's greater participation and input. There is a difference, therefore, in that the former cases all had an agenda outlining the future of women's right and participation while the latter cases were still more focused on just advocating for women's participation in the negotiations. This difference is shaped by these other necessary conditions and the type of access women have to the process and the type of leadership they entail.

Creating access to exclusive processes

The second factor is *access* for women's participation. The condition here is that women must have access to the formal peace process for their agenda to be heard and/or addressed. According to the cases, this access may vary from no access, to indirect or direct access to the process, though as later discussed, in all of these cases women had to *demand* any access to the peace process. In the cases of Guatemala and the DRC, women participated via formal civil society access to the peace processes. In Guatemala, political space and access to the process was secured via the Civil Society Assembly, who were a sanctioned, though indirect, actor during the peace accords. The Assembly had several Sectors and, though women were not initially included, they demanded their inclusion as a separate sector through which they organised and promoted their agenda.[44] In the DRC, women worked through the *forces vives*, which was the civil society sector involved in the ICD.[45] Ultimately, women's participation via civil society resulted in their direct participation in negotiations where women had 40 of 340 seats.[46]

In both Burundi and Uganda, women participated through the granting of 'observer status'. In Burundi, women were able to use this to get all 'nineteen negotiating parties to accept the need for women's involvement in the peace process'.[47] Each of these parties then sent two delegates each to the All-Party Burundi Women's Conference that forged the women's agenda discussed earlier.[48] In Uganda, women also were granted observer status after being initially absent from negotiations. In fact, the Uganda Women's Coalition for Peace was formed in response to women's absence from the process.[49] Women lobbied negotiators

---

[42]'Mindanao People's Caucus Statement of Support.' No date, http://mpc.org.ph/index.php?option=com_content&view=article&id=175:statement-of-support-for-the-appointment-of-two-moro-women-to-the-milf-peace-panel-board-ofconsultants&catid=40:statements&Itemid=15.

[43]Mindanao People's Caucus website, http://mpc.org.ph/documents/gph-milf/10%20Decision%20Points.pdf (accessed June, 2015).

[44]Carillo and Chinchilla, 'From Urban Elite to Peasant Organizing', 146.

[45]Whitman, 'Women and Peace-Building'.

[46]Tripp et al., *African Women's Movements.*

[47]Ibid., 211.

[48]Ibid.

[49]Whitman, 'Women in Peace-Building'.

and, in 2007, approached the UN Envoy with women's concerns about the peace process, ultimately resulting in one women serving on the government negotiation delegation.[50] In this case, women's constant lobbying of, and engagement with, the process directly manufactured access to make their agenda known, but it was more limited than the other cases.

In Darfur, international organisations – notably UNIFEM[51] and the UN – promoted the women's agenda; while women may have demanded access, they depended on mediators for access that was both indirect and not mandated. During the last round of negotiations, a 'Gender Experts Support Team', invited by UNIFEM, Canada, Norway and Finland, actually participated in the peace negotiations after having met with women's groups to form an agenda.[52] These experts were able to then lobby for their inclusion in the process and the DPA includes over 70 sections that refer to women.[53]

In the Philippines, women had both direct and indirect access to the process. As previously stated, MILF appointed two women to its 'peace panel' who engaged in the peace talks, and the government also had at least two women, including a woman as chief negotiator beginning in 2012.[54] MILF's promotion of women for these talks was the first time women had been directly included and this happened as a result of women's activism within the Mindanao People's Caucus (MPC). As in the case of Guatemala, where women worked through a broader coalition of civil society organisations, women organised themselves with the MPC to push them to promote women in MILF, which worked. Thus, while women had been active in the MILF rebel movement, their access to talks was not via the rebel movements but the civil society organisations trying to broker peace.

Based on these cases, we can see how different types of access may have long-term effects for the success of agreements and for the question of who constitutes a stakeholder. When peace processes such as Guatemala, the DRC and the Philippines make access for civil society part of the peace process more generally, this sends an important signal to citizens that they are indeed stakeholders. This may also be beneficial for female activists already working across organisations or issues during the conflict to organise and affect the peace process at early phases. Peace processes that include civil society are less elite events and this may generate more 'buy-in' and awareness among the public in ways that could have long-term ramifications for the success of the process.

Indirect access can also have trade-offs. When women can only 'observe', they may maintain an 'outsider' status that could strengthen their engagement with formal negotiations by maintaining their independence and ability to critique and criticise. Observer status can also be a weak form of access, however, when women want to be heard but have no formal mechanisms to amplify their voices. Also, when women have indirect access, even if it is through a woman-focused organisation such as UN Women, women's participation and representation is always mediated through the organisation, which also has both benefits and costs. The benefits include access to important resources and training women may not otherwise have had. These resources and skills may translate later into women's participation in negotiations and peacebuilding after negotiated settlements. However, it can also mean

---

[50]Ibid.

[51]UNIFEM, or United Nations Development Fund for Women, changed its name in 2011 to UN Women. These are the same organisation, though I use whichever iteration is used in the document or citation.

[52]UNICEF, 'Women and the Darfur Peace Agreement', no date, http://www.unicef.org/sowc07/docs/sowc07_panel_4_3.pdf.

[53]Anne Itto, 'Guests at the Table? The Role of Women in Peace Processes', *Accord* 18 (2006): 56–9.

[54]UN Women, 'Conflict Prevention and Resolution'.

the narratives of what women may want as part of a process is mediated through 'experts', who may use language, ideas and practices less reflective of local women's groups and more reflective of organisational mandates or institutional priorities. This access is then clearly linked to the type of advocacy women may undertake in a peace process.

Advocating for women in peace

The final condition for women's substantive representation in peace agreements is *advocacy*. This means that some combinations of negotiators, mediators, observers and funders are aware of women's concerns and interests and treat them as complementary to other peace demands rather than in competition with them. When women's security demands and substantive representation are considered part and parcel of the issues dealt with in the peace agreement, I call this a complementary process. This is contrasted with competing processes where women's demands are understood as competing with other demands, detracting from process parties major priorities. Complementary processes make it easier for women to both create agendas and have access to peace processes, and competing processes mean women have to find other means to create an agenda and promote it.

A competitive process is illustrated in Sudan's CPA negotiations. One of the female delegates tells the story of how an initial proposal for quotas was dropped because the government refused them, arguing 'they had not been fighting women', so inclusion of provisions for women was not even debatable.[55] In Sudan's case, women were understood only as victims in conflict, not soldiers, leaders or negotiators. This narrow conception of women as victims is both a cause and effect of a competing peace process for women: only those actors who shape and implement these provisions are considered the rightful parties to the negotiation. This was initially the case in the DRC as well, where some of the initial females delegates during the preparatory meetings

> were specifically instructed by their heads of delegations not to promote gender-related issues … when one of the female delegates … stood up to promote protection of women in humanitarian situations, one of the female delegates … stood up to condemn her for wasting time on issues that are not relevant to the ICD process.[56]

Complementary processes result from a spectrum of approaches among parties to the conflict, mediators and the organisations that support the peace process more generally. Despite Sudan's CPA not advocating for women, the outcome for Sudan's Darfur process was quite different. The African Union, which mediated the Darfur process, has a history of promoting women as actual mediators (their delegation to Darfur included women) and promoting women's security in peace processes.[57] Additionally, UNIFEM was able to work directly with the AU to promote the Darfurian women's agenda.[58] While power and wealth sharing were still the most important issues on the table, the DPA process also included human rights, and even began by addressing humanitarian issues. In this sense, even though parties to the conflict were characterised as non-advocates, the mediators were women's advocators and took a complementary approach.

---

[55]Itto, 'Guests at the Table? The Role'.
[56]Whitman, 'Women in Peace-Building'.
[57]UN Women, 'Women's Participation in Peace Negotiations'.
[58]Itto, 'Guests at the Table? The Role'.

BUILDING PEACE

Individual leaders, both men and women, often play an incredibly important role in promoting women's abilities and access to construct, articulate and lobby their objectives, though not always. In Guatemala, Luz Mendez, who was part of the rebel negotiating commission, stated she learned from El Salvador's failure to address women's issues and consciously made it an issue in the commission.[59] She became an important advocate for the Women's Sector, and, as they did not have any formal positions at the actual negotiating table, to have a woman who was at the table meant women's issues had actual representation. Even though the *Unidad Revolucionaria Nacional Guatemalteca* (URNG) did not prioritise women's inclusion, the combination of having an already prepared agenda and indirect access to the process via civil society resulted in a CPA, a more representative and women-friendly peace agreement.[60]

In the DRC, Sir Ketumile, as chief facilitator, engaged women's demands for better representation and worked with UNIFEM to promote more women. Additionally, one of their 'Five Commissions' for resolving conflict – the Humanitarian, Social and Cultural Commission – was headed by Ellen Johnson-Sirleaf.[61] Burundi's process was mediated first by Julius Nyerere and then Nelson Mandela, both of whom engaged women's groups (or at least did not actively banned their participation, even when parties to the conflict tried).[62] In Uganda, leadership minimally promoted a complementary process. In fact, it was more like capitulation to women's insistent demands to participate. The government added one woman to their negotiating delegation at the demand of Uganda Women's Coalition for Peace.[63]

In the Philippines, women's issues were considered complementary to the larger goals of the talks and specifically of MILF. It is apparent the women appointed to MILF negotiating team were there to advocate for other women. Attorney Raissa Jajurie and academic Bai Cabaybay Abukakar were selected during the Women's Conference because of their work as gender advocates.[64] Further, they were selected during a conference on Peace and Security that actively engaged UNSCR 1325, so one can assume their advocacy during the process was to ensure women's interests in the talks and outcomes. The Philippines is one of the few (if only) cases of a female head negotiator, who represented the government. Miriam Coronel-Ferrer was appointed after a long career on peace and conflict studies. While it is not clear whether she specifically advocated for women's issues, there is no indication she impeded it. When Coronel-Ferrer was appointed, there was speculation that MILF may not accept a woman as negotiator (based on ill-founded assumptions about how the Mindanao associate with women), but they released a statement they would accept a chair 'of any gender or ethnicity'.[65]

Persistent barriers for women at the table

Even with this support from international organisations and the strength and tenacity of transnational women's activism and particular women leaders, even these 'best' cases of women's participation in peace processes required a 'fight' from women for their own

---

[59]Luciak, *After the Revolution*.
[60]Ibid.
[61]Whitman, 'Women in Peace-Buidling'.
[62]UN Women, 'Remembering Nelson Mandela's Work to Bring Women to the Table During Peace Talks in Burundi' (2013), http://www.unwomen.org/en/news/stories/2013/12/nelson-mandela-work-in-burundi (accessed January 3, 2016).
[63]Nabukeera-Musoke, 'Transitional Justice and Gender in Uganda', Whitman, 'Women and Peace-Building'.
[64]Statement of Support Mindanao People's Caucus, no date.
[65]Sara Schonhardt, 'Q&A: The Philippines' Peacemaker', *The Wall Street Journal Southeat Asia* (February 10, 2014), http://blogs.wsj.com/searealtime/2014/02/10/qa-the-philippines-peacemaker/.

participation, which has been corroborated by other work.[66] While these findings could be useful for promoting more women in peace processes, some perhaps deeper and troubling issues emerge, including the failure to consider women as central stakeholders during negotiations and how this state of affairs might be challenged.

One example is that of Uganda. The peace agreements explicitly reference UNSCR 1325 and include provisions for all four categories of substantive representation: representation, incorporation, protection and recognition. For all intents and purposes, the process appeared fairly woman-friendly and took seriously the gendered impacts of conflict. But interviews with women who were active in publicising and ending the conflict indicate that what was included was not enough. Harriet Nabukeera-Musoke identified several ways in which peace was 'being forged at the expense of women'. She describes how the women's peace caravan was blamed for the stalled negotiations, how a woman active in the process was accused of having sexual relationships with negotiators, and how the lack of schedule for the talks meant women did not know when and where to be prepared to participate.[67]

In Sudan, women had to slip their suggestions under doors and their claims were marginalised because they apparently had not fought in the war.[68] In the Philippines MILF had never included women in peace talks prior to 2012 peace talks:

> eleven years after the unanimous adoption of the UN Security Resolution 1325 on Women, Peace and Security, the leadership of the Moro Islamic Liberation (MILF) finally responds to the clarion call of women to have active and meaningful participation in the peace talks. This is the first ever known appointment of a Bangsamoro woman in the MILF peace negotiating structures and we salute the MILF peace panel for *finally heeding to the persistent demand and assertion of women.*[69]

During the ICD, women had to demand access to the meeting and create a Plan of Action to make sure gender was included as part of all the ICD commissions.[70] These anecdotes are not isolated events, but rather part of widespread and systematic 'peripherizing' of women during peace processes. And underlying this exclusion is essentialist binary gender logic that problematically categorises women in ways to justify their exclusion. As Geogina Waylen describes it, these institutions of peacebuilding 'are products of gendered power struggles and contestation'.[71] Much of this is informed by the binary thinking of protector-protected, perpetrator-victim and war-peace as they relate to masculinity–femininity, discussed in previous sections.[72]

Conclusion

As the importance of women at the peace table has finally begun to inform policy at the global level, complicating the elements of this participation is essential. This study

---

[66]Waylen, 'A Seat at the Table- Is It Enough?'.

[67]'Transitional Justice and Gender'.

[68]Pablo Castillo Diaz, *Women's Participation in Peace Negotiations: Connections Between Presence and Influence*. UNIFEM, (2010), .http://www.unifem.org/attachments/products/0302_WomensParticipationInPeaceNegotiations_en.pdf.

[69]Mindanao Peoples Caucus, no date, my emphasis.

[70]Whitman, 'Women in Peace-Building'.

[71]Waylen, 'A Seat at the Table- Is It Enough?'.

[72]Helen M, Kinsella, *The Image before the Weapon: A Critical History of the Distinction between Combatant and Civilian*. (New York: Cornell University Press, 2011); Chiseche Salome Mibenge, *Sex and International Tribunals: the Erasure of Gender From the War Narrative* (Philadelphia: University of Pennsylvania Press, 2013); Laura Sjoberg and Caron E. Gentry. *Mothers, Monsters, Whores: Women's Violence in Global Politics* (New York: Zed Books, 2008).

corroborates other recent case study work arguing women's 'presence' alone is not enough to ensure how to get peace.[73] Rather this 'women at the table' discourse must focus on *how* women (and men) participate in peace negotiations. As evidenced by these case studies, women's substantive representation in agreements, measured via UNSCR 1325, is achieved in several ways: women having a specific agenda, preferably written; women's access to the process, preferably formal, direct and multifaceted; and advocacy for women from the powerful actors within the process. As the six cases illustrate, these must be jointly present; the efficacy of women 'at the table' is conditioned by their agenda and advocacy and they have to act on behalf of women in a process that sees women's issues as central to larger objectives. An important place to start is to pressure leaders and international organisations to stop treating peace processes as elite and exclusive events. This affects not only women's access and agency, but the rest of civil society as well. This can have long-term impacts on any success a peace process will have.

What is perhaps most amazing is the agency, creativity and perseverance of women's groups in the face of such blatant discrimination. In other words, women are making their demands heard and getting some demands in peace processes despite the barriers erected to keep them out. Many of the processes listed above include multiple provisions and sections regarding women and conflict, often directly provided by women's groups. Despite the more gender-friendly and woman-aware appearance of these agreements, however, even these best case scenarios of women's inclusion are not enough. While these peace processes appear better than previous processes, there is still a long way to go.

Disclosure statement

No potential conflict of interest was reported by the author.

---

[73]Waylen, 'A Seat at the Table- Is It Enough?'.

The relationship of political settlement analysis to peacebuilding from a feminist perspective

Fionnuala Ní Aoláin[a,b]

[a]Transitional Justice Institute University of Ulster, Belfast, Northern Ireland; [b]University of Minnesota Law School, Minneapolis, MN, USA

ABSTRACT

In the policy literature addressing bilateral state engagement with fragile, conflicted or weakened states, the language of 'political settlement' appears increasingly ubiquitous. But much of the emerging literature is gender blind, and there is little by way of comprehensive scholarly or policy literature available to elucidate the gender dimensions of political settlement. This article explores both how the definition of 'political settlement' functions to include or exclude women both formally and informally, and how emergent 'political settlement' theory and practice can both build on peace agreement analysis and avoid some of its gendered pitfalls. I ask how political settlement analysis works (or does not work) in practice to address women's needs, demands and challenges. Specifically, I explore the kinds of gendered fault lines that have emerged and settled in political settlement practice, and explore insights from law, political science and international relations that might advance women's interests.

The concept of political settlements has entered the mainstream lexicon of peacemaking, political stabilisation and active bilateral engagement with fragile and conflict affected states. Despite its increased pervasiveness in the vocabulary favoured by policy-makers, it has only occasionally surfaced in scholarly literatures.[1] This is in part explained by the interchangeable use of settlement terminology with that of peace agreements, as well as differences in the kinds of ideas, formulations and concepts fashionable in scholarly discourses as distinct from the terminology that comes to dominate policy imperatives at particular points.[2] As the language and framework of political settlement become normalised in the bilateral and multilateral discourses of states and institutions managing conflict, it behoves us to have a better grasp of its meanings and purchase. When language and conceptual frames

---

[1]The term is used by OECD, a number of agencies operating in the humanitarian crisis and development fi elds and by the United Kingdom's Department of International Development (D f ID). See Christine Bell, 'What We Talk About When We Talk About Political Settlements' (working paper, Political Settlements Research Programme, School of Law, University of Edinburgh, 2015).

[2]Organisation for Economic Co-operation and Development. *From Power Struggles to Sustainable Peace: Understanding Political Settlements*. Paris: Organisation for Economic Co-operation and Development, 2011.

shift, so too do political and economic priorities. Thus, attention to political settlement is important to those engaged in peacebuilding and conflict transition in part because new policy priorities deeply affect the messages that key actors and institutions internalise and expect in conflict ending and conflict transition sequencing.

A stable meaning for 'political settlement' remains a work in progress, although the contours of core and penumbra are emerging. For example, the United Kingdom's Department for International Development (DfID) definition of political settlement is a broad one: '…the expression of a common understanding, usually forged between elites, about how power is organised and exercised',[3] and thus the analysis of inclusion and the relevant sites of inquiry is a descriptively broad one. Political settlements have some additional generalisable features. These include the notion that political settlement is a state–society agreement,[4] and that political settlements operate as a two-level game, namely: as a set of interactions and relationships between differently placed elites in reproducing similar dynamics between elites and their followers.[5] One very clear distinction drawn by commentators is that political settlements differ from peace agreements and elite pacts primarily because they are ongoing processes and not one-off events, a contention that is challenged by the sustained analysis of cyclical, sustained, negotiated and renegotiated peace processes (as opposed to peace agreements).[6] At the heart of a loose consensus on the meaning of political settlement is the idea that ending protracted violence in conflict-affected societies mandates engaging and co-opting elite actors with varied alignments of interest-based inducements and incentives. Inclusion conversations and tensions are at the heart of this discourse.[7] Not surprisingly, an emphasis on inclusivity raises the spectre of transformative political space in which women will be present on equal terms. Whether political settlement can deliver any better on that promise than other arenas have (e.g. peace-agreements or the United Nations Women, Peace and Security agenda), is an open question, partially explored in this article.

As the traction of political settlement increases, the term has broadly been assumed gender blind and there is little by way of comprehensive analysis available to elucidate the gendered nature and form of political settlement. There are relevant and overlapping literatures, namely: gender and peace agreement literature,[8] feminist analysis of political participation and political process by women,[9] a very recent body of gender and statebuilding literature,[10] and a broad conflict management literature that to a lesser or greater degree

---

[3]Department for International Development. *Building Peaceful States and Societies*. London: Department for International Development, 2010. It is worth noting the context of DfID's use of the terminology that there is a tangible link between peace and statebuilding through the prism of political settlement.

[4]Verena Fritz and Alina Rocha Menocal, *Understanding State-building from a Political Economy Perspective: An Analytical and Conceptual Paper on Processes, Embedded Tensions and Lessons for International Engagement* (London: Overseas Development Institute, 2007).

[5]Edward Laws, *Political Settlements, Elite Pacts, and Governments of National Unity: A Conceptual Study* (Birmingham: Developmental Leadership Program, 2012), 9.

[6]Ibid., 21. However, peace process analysis would dispute the characterisation of peace processes as one-off events, and equally stress the long-term process-based nature of the peace agreement context. Christine Bell, *On the Law of Peace: Peace Agreements and the Lex Pacificatoria* (Oxford: Oxford University Press, 2008).

[7]Corresponding to the emergence of 'vertical integration' discourses in peacebuilding literature. See Erin Mccandless, Eric Abitbol and Timothy Donais, 'Vertical Integration: A Dynamic Practice Promoting Transformative Peacebuilding', special issue, *Journal of Peacebuilding & Development* 10 (2015): 1–9.

[8]Fionnuala Ní Aoláin, Naomi Cahn and Dina Haynes, *On the Frontlines: Gender, War and the Post-conflict Process* (Oxford: Oxford University Press, 2011).

[9]Aili Tripp and others, *African Women's Movements: Transforming Political Landscapes* (Cambridge: Cambridge University Press, 2009).

[10]Organisation for Economic Co-operation and Development. *Gender and Statebuilding in Fragile and Conflict Affected States*. Paris: Organisation for Economic Co-operation and Development, 2013.

includes references to women. Evident is the conceptual and practical overlap with the Women, Peace and Security agenda where normative content places an exceptionally high value on the inclusion of women in all dimensions of conflict prevention, negotiation and enforcement.[11] However, critical thinking is required to understand how the definition of 'political settlement' functions to include or exclude women both formally and informally, and how dynamics of gender power, inequality and access function in this arena.

The presumption that 'political settlement' operates as a category that includes and embraces women's needs must be critically interrogated from the outset. We need to better understand how and to what degree the emerging practices of political settlement come with well-established gender norms, what precisely these norms involve and how such embedded ways of doing things could be modified or corrected to take greater account of the needs of women in negotiations from conflict or repression involving both state and non-state actors. This is particularly important as the degree of overlap between political settlement framing and peacebuilding narrows. Given that much policy and scholarly work has been invested in mainstreaming women in the negotiation, mediation and implementation of peace processes, there is a certain paradox when the concepts, framing and tools change and/or donors and institutional actors decide to adopt a different vocabulary to capture and frame change processes and in the course of this, women somehow metaphorically and practically fall out.

In tracking the relationship between political settlement and peacebuilding, this article starts by giving a brief overview of the concept and emerging practices of political settlement, highlighting points of interface with the established fields of peacebuilding and/or peace processes. I trace its roots and development, tracking how overview of the intellectual roots of the field reveals the masculinity of its origins and the infused patriarchy of its practices. Part two draws on a range of feminist theorising and particularly on feminist institutionalism to demonstrate the institutional practices that limit the scope of women's engagement in the schema of political settlement and peacemaking as currently conceived. It reminds us that political settlement is not an alien planet, and that many of the gendered dynamics of power/exclusion, violence/insecurity, invisibility/outsider and access/marginalisation are true for women across a range of contested political contexts. I conclude that both formal and informal institutional barriers define the universe of women's engagements in the peace and security domain and that the shift to new discourses requires an investment by scholars, practitioners and advocates to expose, agitate and affirm the exclusions and limitations in this new terrain without losing sight of what we have learnt in our travels through other parallel domains. Part three seeks to identify a way forward and a tentative re-visioning of this emerging field.

The roots of political settlement – where we are and where we came from

The emerging literature on political settlement includes multiple country studies (e.g. Cambodia, India, South Africa and a number of other historical cases).[12] Here, I am particularly concentrated on political settlement in sites of conflict and/or in sites emerging from

---

[11]See UN Security Council Resolution 1325, S/RES/1325; Fumi Olonisakin, Karen Barnes and Eka Ikpe, *Women, Peace and Security: Translating Policy into Practice* (London: Routledge, 2010); Laura J. Shepherd, *Gender, Violence and Security: Discourse as Practice* (London: Zed Books, 2008).

[12]See Laws, *Political Settlements, Elite Pacts, and Governments of National Unity.*

political repression. A political settlement in these places is quintessentially an agreement reached by process of political engagement, negotiation, mediation and barter between parties who have previously been in dispute, often violently. To understand political settlement and its contemporary usage, we are aware that the disputes concerned are intensely rooted in sectarian, ethnic, ideological, resource-defined, territorial and cultural difference. Those differences have frequently culminated in a politics propped up and enabled by violence. That violence is frequently (though not necessarily) located in ethno-national masculine discourses where gendered nationalism invariably marginalises women by exalting 'armed patriarchy'.[13] The violence is often long term, cyclical, highly disparate in its forms and invariably destructive of civilian lives, civilian infrastructure and the civility that enables diverse humanity to thrive in political communities.

Specific forms of gender-based violence and situated gendered harms follow from these conflict typologies for women.[14] During conflict, women directly experience various impacts, many related to sexual violence, including unwanted pregnancies, sexually transmitted diseases and community stigma. Given the strictures of community and socially determined family roles, the impact of economic devastation, forced displacement, health deterioration and loss of education falls in highly gender-stratified ways on women and girls. There is increasing recognition that gendered harms are insufficiently captured by the narrow rubric of sexual harm and that gender-relevant conflict effects encompass a range of economic, social and political dimensions. These include limited employment, maternal harms, dire health outcome, short-, medium- and long-term loss of schooling and training, forced migration, restricted mobility and a plethora of cultural impairments occasioned by conflict.

Political settlements capture the solution to transcending these profound barriers of violence, othering and dysfunction the solution as forging 'a common understanding, usually between political elites, that their best interests are served through acquiescence to a framework of administering political power'.[15] But the preference for political settlement does not really explain how different types of political settlement emerge or the actors, institutions, resources and practices that shape them. Moreover, we have a limited understanding of how political settlement can be improved by internally driven initiatives, including the impact of gender-inclusive processes and rule of law institutions. It remains unclear whether political settlement is per se unable to address gendered lacunae that have emerged in peace process, reconstruction and state-building discourses. And, of course, political settlements do not emerge in a vacuum. In particular, international elites play a critical role in shaping the kind of political settlement that emerges based on the form, layering and continuity of intervention that is directed towards a society in conflict.

The concentrated value placed in political settlement discourse on elite engagement has some very obvious constraints for gender analysis. This affirms the fundamental inquiry of this article, namely: what kinds of gendered fault line have emerged and settled in political

---

[13]Monica McWilliams, 'Struggling for Peace and Justice: Reflections on Women's Activism in Northern Ireland', *Journal of Women's History* 6, no. 7 (1995): 15; Kris Brown and Fionnuala Ní Aoláin, 'Through the Looking Glass: Transitional Justice Futures through the Lens of Nationalism, Feminism and Transformative Change', *International Journal of Transitional Justice* 1 (2015): 127.

[14]Aisling Swaine, 'Beyond Strategic Rape and Between the Public and Private: Violence Against Women in Armed Conflict', *Human Rights Quarterly* 3 (2015): 37.

[15]Jonathan Di John and James Putzel, *Political Settlements: Issue Paper* (Birmingham: Governance and Social Development Resource Centre, 2009), 94.

settlement practice.[16] It goes without saying that understanding the role of elites should not foreclose the complexity of contending elites, inter-elite bargaining and, in particular, the shifting and sometime tenuous status of elites in ever-combustible conflict sites. But in reflecting further on the centrality of elite engagement in political settlement processes, one ultimately contends with the insider/outsider dynamics that are manifest when advantage accrues consistently to system insiders, those with accumulated military prowess and the in-built historical advantages of racial, wealth and property benefits in existing status quo orders.[17] The overlap of concentrations of power with a gender order is indisputable and has gone hand in hand with the exclusion of women from exercising political, economic and social power in a broad range of societal contexts.[18] However, gender exclusion is not our only challenge. Equally concerning is the selective inclusion of elite women whose claims to presence may rest on their indisputable relationship to an elite powerful man (or men in clan-based systems) which may disguise the unrestrained entrenchment of a masculine world view with the veneer of female legitimacy. The presence of even a small number of (uncompromised) women in the negotiation, mediation and barter space underscores a singular problem identified by British feminist sociologist Carol Smart 'of challenging a form of power without accepting its own terms of reference and hence losing the battle before it has begun'.[19]

The emphasis on strategies to engage and maintain the 'buy-in' of elites dominates political settlement literature.[20] And while peacebuilding literature does not overtly place the same kind of sustained emphasis on elite buy-in, peace process practice is deeply influenced by the imperative of maintaining the goodwill of elite actors, particularly the military participants in conflict. The emphasis on elites *ab initio* serves to exclude women whose political, economic and social capital is consistently lesser than men. The necessity of co-opting elites also has substantive crossover with the literatures that emerged in the early 1970s and since addressing transitionary compacts in authoritarian settings. It appeared early in the formative work of political theorists O'Donnell and Schmitter, and has been followed through by Diamond and Linz among others.[21] Core to this component of political settlement literature is the importance of 'elite pacts', the value placed on the 'skills, values, strategies and choices' of elites and the positive disposition of elites which helps make a consolidated democracy work.[22] Little, if any, attention has been paid to the masculinities of these elite actors, the exclusionary politics which produces them and the implication for gender relations of the 'buck' stopping with elite, generally militarised men. My prior work has reflected on the gender-based cooperation between seemingly oppositional elite men whose patriarchal instincts are generally well aligned,[23] and the resulting political alignments that protect

---

[16]Ibid. The authors identify the work of Mushtaq Khan as the most theoretically robust work emerging from the field of historical political economy.

[17]For a powerful decolonial analysis of these dynamics in transitional settings, see Pascha Bueno-Hansen, 'Engendering Transitional Justice: Reflections on the Case of Peru', *Journal of Peacebuilding* 5, no. 3 (2010): 5.

[18]Carole Pateman, *The Sexual Contract* (Redwood City, CA: Stanford University Press, 1988), 182.

[19]Carol Smart, *Feminism and the Power of Law* (London: Routledge, 1989), 5.

[20]John Higley and Richard Gunther, *Elites and Democratic Consolidation in Latin America and Southern Europe* (Cambridge: Cambridge University Press, 1992); Guillermo O'Donnell and Philippe C. Schmitter, *Transitions from Authoritarian Rule: Tentative Conclusions About Uncertain Democracies* (Baltimore, MD: Johns Hopkins University Press, 1986).

[21]Guillermo O'Donnell and Philippe C. Schmitter, *Transitions from Authoritarian Rule: Tentative Conclusions about Uncertain Democracies*, (Baltimore. MD: Johns Hopkins University Press, 2013), 65–72; Larry Diamond and others, eds., *Democracy in Developing Countries: Latin America* (Boulder, CO: Lynne Rienner, 1989).

[22]Diamond and others, eds., *Democracy in Developing Countries*, 14.

[23]Fionnuala Ní Aoláin, 'Women, Security, and the Patriarchy of Internationalized Transitional Justice', *Human Rights Quarterly* 4 (2009): 31.

masculine benefits and ill-serve women's interests. Paying closer attention to seemingly liberal but de facto retrograde gendered pacts producing political settlements that poorly serve women in the spheres of reproductive rights, the regulation of violence, access to economic goods on equal terms and the advancement of both substantive and procedural equality for women are markers of our route to gender benchmarking political settlements.

Given the consequences of concentrating elite power and negotiation in political settlement processes, it would seem that close attention to patronage and clientelist politics is also necessary to fully understand the limits on women's political effectiveness and the state's accountability. We increasingly appreciate that women are side-lined in formal political negotiation processes (whether 'one-off', stop-start or continuous political adaptations) that are defined by constant bartering over conflict ending. Moreover, there are some self-evident obstacles that follow from supporting and prioritising embedded relationships that are culturally, socially and historically male. Goetz and Jenkins' gender-focused study of these insider and insidious politics underscores the necessity of unpacking the gender impact of clientelist and patronage-based politics. These politics constitute direct barriers to enabling women's meaningful engagement with and influence upon negotiation processes.[24]

Moreover, in revealing the centrality of clientelist relationships to the production and maintenance of elite stratification in conflicted societies, we should pay close attention to the public/private divide that has historically concentrated women's social and political capital (such as it is) in the private, unregulated sphere of family and clan, and women's exclusion from the public sphere where power is exercised. Barriers that exclude or limit women's access to the public sphere, holding them to the 'sticky floor and glass ceiling', mean that in real terms, women's capacity to develop clientelist and patronage relationships, instrumentally necessary to the exercise of power, will be functionally sealed off.[25]

Feminist insight, Political settlement and Feminist method

How have political settlements worked in practice to address women's needs, demands and challenges? What women and what kinds of interests are included in political settlement processes? Do these women resemble the 'elite' actors that figure so prominently in political settlement conceptualisation? What kinds of gendered barriers exist both to inclusion and to influence the determination of 'substantive' content for negotiation? To illuminate these questions, my analysis in this section is focused on the available tools that have defined feminist engagement in peace and security as well as institutional analysis. Above all, I employ what Cynthia Enloe describes as a 'feminist curiosity' about the ways in which outcomes and institutional preferences serve the dynamic and shifting power relationships of elite male actors (and their followers) but rarely operate in service to the needs and dynamic interests of women.[26]

How have women tried to affect both the formal and informal 'rules of the game' as to influence how power is held and exercised to their benefit? How and where do women 'fit' within an analysis of elite bargaining? What strategies have women used to try to impact

---

[24]Anne-Marie Goetz and Robert Jenkins, *Reinventing Accountability: Making Democracy Work for Human Development* (New York: Palgrave, 2005).

[25]Susan Boyd, *Challenging the Public/Private Divide: Feminism, Law, and Public Policy* (Toronto: University of Toronto Press, 1997).

[26]Cynthia Enloe, *Bananas, Beaches and Bases: Making Feminist Sense of International Politics* (Berkeley: University of California Press, 2014), 241.

political settlements to be more inclusive? What do women's gains tell us about the 'wider process of bargaining between elites'? Not all of these questions are answered in this article, which primarily opens up their relevance to political settlement analysis.

Answering these questions involves closely examining the exercise of power in complex political negotiations via analyses of power provided in political settlement and peace negotiation literature. Theoretically, there is a sufficiently comprehensive notion that both the 'power' to be organised and the 'elites' to do the work in political settlement are expansively open. For example, commentators have posited that one cannot determine how inclusive or exclusionary a political settlement is '[s]imply by looking at the extent of the participation in the bargaining process, or at appointments in the offices of the state', but rather the openness of settlement can only be gauged by engaging in a broader analysis of 'the distribution of rights and entitlements across groups and classes in society on which the settlement is based'.[27] Moreover, the literature assumes that political settlements are adaptable processes, responsive to social needs and social demands.[28] Despite this optimism on the malleability of power and the capacity to 'move the deckchairs' with ease, feminist analysis reveals the gendered dimensions in the existing organisation of power relationships in society. Unfailingly, the definition of elites in most societal contexts is masculine in form and in representation. Feminist analysis consistently underscores the intractability of enabling transformative political change when patriarchal power is engaged. Feminists identify the narrowness of the entry points for women to claim a reordering of social norms and institutions whose practices disadvantage them on the basis of gender.[29] Moreover, the emphasis on the role of elites assumes a top-down (distinctly not bottom-up) approach and the concept clearly inherits the gender hierarchies and biases embedded in all social arrangements and institutions organised in a hierarchical manner (with the obvious historical and/or colonial baggage that accompanies such ordering). Harkening back to the well-trodden ground of gendering power and recalling the rigidity of gendered relations are a cogent reminder that political settlement is no more exempt from the general analysis than are other institutional sites in which power is divided, managed and exercised. Women's demands, needs and challenges face a host of familiar barriers to engagement and benefit in this area as well as site-specific challenges that follow from the specificity of geographical and political contexts in which political settlements are being pursued. These barriers, including the overarching challenges of exclusion from both formal and informal institutional power, explain in part why women consistently lag behind in their access to peacemaking and conflict resolution spaces.

Understanding exclusion better: intersectionality

Thus, a core inquiry of this article is what women and what kinds of interests are included and excluded in political settlement processes? Intersectionality analysis provides us with the tools to address the questions of beneficiaries and losers in the political negotiation and gains game. Drawing on core feminist method usefully advances an investigation of

---

[27] Jonathan Di John and James Putzel, *Political Settlements: Issue Paper*, 5.

[28] Alan Whaites, 'States in Development: Understanding State-Building' (working paper, Department for International Development, London, 2008), 7.

[29] Anne Bottomley and Joanne Conaghan, 'Feminist Theory and Legal Strategy', special issue, *Journal of Law and Society* 20, no. 1 (2015): 1.

political settlement as a form of public legal and political power operating within well-defined gender tropes. An additional tool that helpfully intersects with a feminist 'take' on political settlement is the conceptual framework of intersectionality. Intersectionality was pioneered as an analytical tool to scrutinise how the most marginalised women's experience of harm,[30] in the workplace and the home, was occluded within the institutions responsible for legal remedy and protection.[31] Intersectionality brings the most marginalised women's lives into the conversation and centres our analysis on the social distribution of political gains, with particular relevance to conflicted and post-conflict societies.[32] As Rooney and Swaine perceptively note:

> Intersectionality provides important conceptual tools that highlight the limitations of 'gender' as a single analytical category. It enables us to understand the gendered and class dimensions of social identities in politically divided societies whilst providing a way out of the impasses of 'identity politics. [33]

In the context of conflicted and fragile states, an intersectional analysis enables exposure of how, despite the systematic harms and exclusions experienced by women, negotiation, mediation and barter processes consistently fail to address or remedy their needs.[34] Intersectionality helps us understand why, despite an increasingly strident rhetoric validating inclusion for women in peace agreement negotiations, and a remarkable emphasis on representation for women in the WPS agenda, negotiations consistently fall short in the adequacy of their representation and reproduce class, ethnic, religious and patriarchial hierarchies even as they portend to dismantle the barriers to inclusion for women.[35]

Intersectionality also provides a nuanced tool to more fully assesses the gendered politics of political representation, and the ways in which women are both present (and not) in the elite settings which are central to political settlement and even when present have less traction than their physical presence in the negotiation space might suggest.[36] Given the paucity of women's representation in political settlement arenas, intersectionality analysis forces us to ask whom does the 'woman' who is present represent? The 'add women and stir' solution persists, as does the persistent tendency to validate the inclusion of women who replicate the elite social, economic and political status of the men who are present in negotiations. Thus, if woman becomes a code for 'doing' inclusion better, it disappoints precisely because sex alone fails to capture the complexities of women's situated political positions in violent societies. Despite the demonstrated essentialism of female inclusion in many peace processes and its cornerstone status in the Women, Peace and Security agenda, the core lesson has yet to be learnt. Namely, that it is precisely the complex marbling of women's lives that requires meaningful representation, both to do justice to women and to undo the proven limitations of elite bargains for women.

---

[30]Kimberlé Crenshaw, 'Intersectionality and Identity Politics: Learning from Violence against Women of Color', in *The Public Nature of Private Violence*, eds. Martha Albertson Fineman and Rixanne Mykitiuk (New York: Routledge, 1991), 178–93.

[31]Patricia Hill Collins, 'Some Group Matters: Intersectionality, Situated Standpoints, and Black Feminist Thought", in *Feminist Frontiers*, eds. Laurel Richardson and Verta (Boston: McGraw-Hill, 2004), 66–84.

[32]Fionnuala Ní Aoláin and Eilish Rooney, 'Underenforcement and Intersectionality: Gendered Aspects of Transitional for Women', *International Journal of Transitional Justice* 1 (2007): 383.

[33]Eilish Rooney and Aisling Swaine, 'The 'Long Grass' of Agreements: Promise, Theory and Practice', special issue, *International Criminal Law Review: Special Issue: Transitional Justice and Restorative Justice* 10, no. 12 (2012): 519–48.

[34]Aisha Nicole Davis, 'Intersectionality and International Law: Recognizing Complex Identities on the Global Stage', *Harvard Human Rights Journal*. 28 (2013): 205–42.

[35]See Kathy Davis, 'Intersectionality as Buzzword: A Sociology of Science Perspective on What Makes a Feminist Theory Successful', *Feminist Theory* 9 (2008): 69.

[36]Fionnuala Ní Aoláin and Eilish Rooney, 'Underenforcement and Intersectionality: Gendered Aspects of Transition for Women'.

In contrast to peace agreement discourses, political settlement has no such gender inclusion mantra. Rather, the language and emphasis on inclusivity has remained buried in the landfill of moving out from narrowly defined elite spaces to broader societal (read also civil society) engagement in political settlement processes. Of course, there is invariably a danger that a fast move on gender inclusivity will happen by simply 'adding women and stirring' in the political settlement literature and practice, which has been the highway taken by the peacemaking cavalry. We should not be under any illusions that adding the mere presence of some women in these negotiation spaces constitutes a radical break with the core of political settlement practice which remains definitively fixed on elite (male) actors. Attention to intersectionality in practice would allow for the possibility of moving us beyond elite narrow bands of female representation, revealing a deeper swathe of women's (and men's) experiences relevant to the deeper purchase of political settlement by those often affected the most by conflict. Shallow representation is likely to overwhelmingly exclude experiences of sustained collective and familial harm that define violent communal hostilities over protracted periods for many.

Lest we forget, one powerful contribution of feminist theorising in the peace and security arena in recent years has been a sustained emphasis on the power, resilience and agency of female actors in conflict.[37] This theorising is highly relevant to engaging women in political settlement theory and practice. This shift to acknowledge and affirm agency has been deliberate. It comes with increased public recognition of the costs that follow from conflict for women, and a highly politicised emphasis on protecting women from sexual violence in armed conflict settings.[38] There is no doubt that the protective move in peace and security discourses has had important symbolic and practical benefits for women.[39] However, when the only gendered move in the peace and security arena is to protective politics, the broader imperatives of inclusion, participation and action become muted, thereby ceding political settlement power to male actors. Agency analysis deepens our understanding of the intersectional roles women play during conflict as victims, participants, bystanders and combatants, thereby complicating the picture of female engagement in and experience of sustained conflict and fragility in state settings. It also brings a broader set of political and military interests to the table, redefining military and female space in the process. With a more nuanced understanding of the complexity of roles that women play in conflict, we are better placed to speculate about how women can and will be engaged in political settlement processes.

Agency analysis also interacts with intersectional approaches to female participation. It is essential to assess the ways in which the women who are present in negotiations function and what their leeway to engage on particular issues may be. To date, participation analysis tends to be hogtied to the notion that ordinary women (and even those extraordinary women who make it through to negotiation space) can shift polarity or overpower embedded patriarchy if only given access.[40] Extensive empirical data are limited, but anecdotal evidence

---

[37]Laura Sjoberg and Caron Gentry, *Mothers, Monsters, Whores: Women's Violence in Global Politics* (London: Zed Books, 2007).

[38]The most high-profile dimensions of this protective move are captured by the series of UN Security Council Resolutions addressing conflict-related sexual violence beginning with Resolution 1325.

[39]Dianne Otto, 'The Exile of Inclusion: Reflections on Gender Issues in International Law Over the Last Decade', *Melbourne Journal of International Law* 10 (2009).

[40]Catherine O'Rourke, 'Walk[ing] the Halls of Power? Understanding Women's Participation in International Peace and Security' *Melbourne Journal of International Law* 15 (2014).

suggests the very limited spaces that open for women in focused negotiated settings as well as in longer span, political accommodation processes are highly constrained.[41] Women are hampered in seen and unseen ways by both formal and informal institutional practices as well as the capacity of patriarchal assumptions and values to pervade seemingly brand new negotiation settings.

Naming masculinities and hierarchies in political settlement

Addressing the intersection of gender and security in the context of political settlement can be challenging. In particular, the relevance of masculinity, male status and hierarchy has both local and international resonance, with direct consequences for the inclusion and exclusion of women from political negotiations. For example, Cockburn and Zarkov have argued '[t]hat the post-conflict environment, like conflict, is vividly about male power systems, struggles and identity formation'.[42] Moreover, there may be an enormous flux in that male post-conflict fraternity, both on an individual and communal level. Men who were in power are losing power, other men are taking their places and, as is often the case when conflict stalemate arises, internationals (generally culturally – and politically differentiated other males) are coming into societies to fill vacuums. As Handrahan has noted, this 'international fraternity' – the community of decision-makers and experts who arrive after a conflict on a mission of 'good will' – holds the upper hand, morally, economically and politically.[43] However, while the international presence is lauded for rescuing such societies from the worst of their own excesses, what is little appreciated is that such men also bring with them varying aspects of gender norms and patriarchal behaviour that transpose into the vacuum they fill, including modalities of sexual violation.[44]

Moreover, despite an array of cultural differences between locals and internationals, what is frequently overlooked are the fundamentally similar patriarchal views that internal and external elites share, which operate in tandem to exclude, silence or nullify women's needs from the political settlement space.[45] As Zarkov and Cockburn explore in their edited collection, the loosening of rigid gender roles from the social flux that conflict inevitably creates is not necessarily sealed off at a conflict's end or the prospect of political settlement by national male leadership. Rather, this role is taken up by the male international development community, 'whose own sense of patriarchy-as-normal is quite intact'.[46]

Thus, the role of local and international elites in setting the framework for settlement and the relationship of security (or lack thereof) is an important dimension framing how women experience political settlement in real time. It may also be critical to understand why so many political settlements fail for lack of legitimacy. We should note the prescient reality

---

[41]Kathleen Staudt, 'Gender Politics in Bureaucracies: Theoretical Issues in Comparative Perspective', in *Women, International Development, and Politics: The Bureaucratic Mire*, ed. Kathleen Staudt (Philadelphia, PA: Temple University Press, 1997), 4.

[42]Lori Handrahan, 'Conflict, Gender, Ethnicity and Post-conflict Reconstruction', *Security Dialogue* 35 (2004): 433, citing Cynthia Cockburn and Dubravka Zarkov, eds., *The Postwar Moment: Militaries, Masculinities and International Peacekeeping* (London: Lawrence and Wishart, 2002).

[43]Lori Handrahan, 'Conflict, Gender, Ethnicity and Post-conflict Reconstruction', 433.

[44]See Lesley Abdela, 'Kosovo: Missed Opportunities, Lessons for the Future', *Development in Practice* 13, nos. 2–3 (2003): 208. Abdela, the former Deputy Director for Democratisation for the OSCE Mission in Kosovo, details the consistent lack of integration of women and gender-related issues into the planning of the Interim Arrangements for Kosovo.

[45]Fionnuala Ní Aoláin, Women, Security and the Patriarchy of Internationalized Transitional Justice', 31 *Human Rights Quarterly* 1055 (2009).

[46]Lori Handrahan, 'Conflict, Gender, Ethnicity and Post-conflict Reconstruction', 436.

that post-conflict sites enable local (previously oppositional) elites to come together, and that a consolidation point often is perversely the oppression of women. This point has been cogently illustrated by the regressive politics of reproductive rights in political settlement processes in societies as diverse as Chile, Northern Ireland and Poland. Paradoxically, the process of consolidating and uniting elites has emboldened conservative forces in many fragile and post-conflict states, reinvigorating their moral and social claims and creating new platforms and legitimate claim spaces to press such positions as bargaining chips in wider political settlement bargaining.

How might peacemaking and political settlement function to include women's needs and interests?

Identifying the flaws of peacemaking and political settlement mechanisms only gets us a little bit down the road to reimagining different ways to produce tolerable settlements that do not merely end violence but address the causalities that produce the violence in the first place.[47] Knowing the fault lines and understanding the challenges that women face in political settlement contexts are only a tentative first step to deeper, more transformative politics in conflicted societies.[48] The more salient question is how to create processes that move societies past structural chauvinism, unpredictable yet sustained violence, the perpetuation of sharp inequalities and the loss of civic trust. Furthermore, political settlement constitutes, in an echo of Mushtaq Khan's early pre-occupations, a primary vehicle to improve economic capacity and human well-being, echoing the call of feminist scholars to centralise social and economic protections and well-being in conflict and post-conflict settings.[49] Transformative political settlement may not only be better politics in the narrow sense of the term but provides the foundations from which economic growth, economic inclusion and sustainable development are fully integrated in and enabled by women's equality and autonomy.

One challenge, given the acceptance that women have been excluded from elite-driven processes, is how to address the conceptual and methodological challenges that create sites of resistance to the inclusion of women in political settlement processes.[50] These processes are in part the product of the 'liberal peace'.[51] To venture to include women means working up against the logic of modernity to make sense of experiences, communities and ways of doing which are significantly outside the scope of what can be imagined and understood in the prevailing order. They are also in part the product of messy 'hybrid political orders' which follow from the clash of the liberal peace and local resistance to it through informal spaces and processes. In particular, the anchors of the liberal peace, individualism, linear temporality and binary logic 'devalue other ways of knowing, including relational logic

---

[47]This avoids what Edward Laws has termed 'unresponsive' settlements. See Edward Laws. *Political Settlements, Elite Pacts*, 27.

[48]Elements of this approach have already been articulated in the transitional justice field, see e.g. Paul Gready and Simon Robins, 'From Transitional to Transformative Justice: A New Agenda for Practice' *The International Journal of Transitional Justice*, 1 (2014): 1–23; Fionnuala Ní Aoláin, Catherine O'Rourke and Aisling Swaine 'Transforming Reparations for Conflict-related Sexual Violence: Principles and Practice' *Harvard Human Rights Journal* 97 (2015): 98.

[49]Fionnuala Ní Aoláin, Naomi Cahn and Dina Haynes, *On the Frontlines: Gender, War and the Post-conflict Process*.

[50]International Center for Transitional Justice. Confronting Impunity and Engendering Transitional Justice Processes in Northern Uganda. New York: International Center for Transitional Justice. Confronting Impunity and Engendering Transitional Justice Processes in Northern Uganda, 2014.

[51]In this critique, the liberal peace constitutes an imposed agenda, which is a poor fit for local legal and political cultures contributing to instability in post-conflict societies.

based on collectivity'.[52] The ambiguity about harnessing women's interest to political settlement/peace agreement processes is underpinned by a deep discomfort with rectifying race, class and gender inequalities.[53]

The goal then is a transformative project. It will not be fulfilled by tinkering with inclusionary rules, more consistently setting aside a couple of random seats at negotiation tables, or appointing more connected and acceptable women to sit on the new (or revitalised) institutional bodies that advance the enforcement dimensions of political settlement. It requires sustained attention to and remedy of institutional exclusions and privileges (formal and informal), and intentionality to intersectional identity plus a deep reach beyond the easy representation offered by the woman who fits in easily. I underscore that the move to transformative politics is partly enabled by the ferocity of violence that prompts the move to settlement politics in the first place. Thus, our departure point is an understanding that a saturation point for violence is interwoven with the endogenous and exogenous pressures to negotiate. Political settlement, to avoid the fault lines of peace agreement logic, demands thinking beyond the revulsion of immediate overwhelming violence, with an eye to deeper insecurities and causalities. Avoiding the heady impulse of the quick fix is another imperative.

Oddly, some of the core tenets of peace agreements function directly relational to the violence of conflict. Specifically, the imperative to end violence prioritises the inclusion of military actors. Sequentially, the desire to keep them in bargaining space often means a set of compromises are made that limit the broader and longer term transformative aspects of the peace deal. Those compromises frequently work least well for women, who are generally unlikely to be in the military camp and whose inclusion or exclusion from bargaining processes is generally not viewed as central to delivering or maintaining the deal. The past 15 years of claims to include women in making peace through the Women Peace and Security mandate are based on arguments of fairness, representation and more recently, the hope that a 'better' deal may emerge.[54] The challenge here is that the essentialism necessary to undergird that claim presumes that the woman who is present is inherently gender-attuned in her ambition and representation.[55] The data reveal this presumption to be inherently flawed.[56] Nonetheless, the argument for inclusion ought not to be based on a higher standard of quality representation for women than we demand of the men. Such a position would be self-defeating and inherently unsound. Minimally, women should be proportionally present in the critical spaces of negotiation, mediation and barter around conflict-ending sequences, the substance of the deal itself, and in all the micro spaces of negotiation that follow security sector reform, from economic development to constitution writing.

One clear takeaway is to view thresholds of violence as necessary scaffolding and sometimes a straightjacket to both political settlement and peacemaking processes. It is a very hard task to disaggregate the power secreted by violence (or its threat) at the peace table.

---

[52]Pascha Bueno-Hansen, 'Engendering Transitional Justice: Reflections on the Case of Peru', 62.

[53]Ratna Kapur, *Erotic Justice: Law and the New Politics of Post-Colonialism* (London: Glasshouse Press, 2005), 17.

[54]Dina Haynes, Naomi Cahn and Fionnuala Ní Aoláin, 'Women in the Post Conflict Process: Reviewing the Impact of Recent U.N. Actions in Achieving Gender Centrality', *Santa Clara Journal of International Law* 11 (2012); Fionnuala Ní Aoláin, Naomi Cahn and Dina Haynes, *On the Frontlines: Gender, War and the Post-conflict Process*, 12.

[55]Ní Aoláin and others, *On the Frontlines*, 140–41.

[56]Christine Bell and Catherine O'Rourke, 'Peace Agreements or Pieces of Paper? The Impact of UNSC Resolution 1325 on Peace Processes and their Agreements', *International and Comparative Law Quarterly*, 59 (2010): 941–80.

No easy solution can be offered here, but a more caustic recognition of the violence–power entanglement and the downstream consequences of maintaining rather than undermining violently sourced male power through the process of deal-making ought to provide sufficient incentive to mediators. If nothing else, the prospect of 'groundhog day' negotiations could encourage producing procedural and substantive institutions and mechanisms that create a fissure between military might and the maintenance of choked political power.[57] It ought to be obvious that if political settlements merely retain entrenched patriarchial violence by other means, the advancement of multicultural coexistence and the mutuality of interests across identities have not moved very far.

Here, a number of safeguards are proposed. First is a deceptively simple proposition that the table itself must be bigger and deeper to accord representation to a wider array of actors. This is not a new silver bullet. Feminist peace scholars and other critics of the liberal peace have consistently argued for diversity and inclusion in peace processes. Their claim to intersectional representation is one that ought to be treated seriously. It is a claim that has equal resonance in political settlement discourses. Inclusion is a not a new word for political settlement and has been used as a way to explain the stability and legitimacy in configuring long-lasting and broadly functional political systems.[58] But the emphasis on inclusivity for feminist scholars clearly means something different than stability and durability of political settlement within the terms of current policy debates. Stability and durability can simply mean that the men with guns continue to run the show and that the 'trains run on time'. In a transformed polity, stability is inherently connected to gender security. The durability of the settlement is pegged to deep support from diverse (read intersectional) political, social and economic communities and particularly marked by the support of the most vulnerable and marginalised in society. This upends the traditional markers of elite satisfaction with the status quo as the basis for comfort in the security of the deal.

Second, a key practice is gendered agency, and the goal that political settlement processes enable and promote agency for women. This is all good in theory, but we have to be very careful of the process by which it is achieved. Specifically 'giving women voice presumes that these women were/are mute'.[59] From this, I infer that the failure to give sufficient voice to women in existing processes should not be taken to confirm that female activism and engagement are absent in the daily doing of politics in the conflicted site. In transforming political settlement, there is peripheral awareness that women's engagement exists and is present at multiple levels in deeply conflicted societies. However, harnessing it on its own terms is a necessity to provide sustenance and long-term viability to inclusively based political processes. Connected is the more existential methodological question of whether women are really 'outside' or how the external international gaze understands 'outsider' and 'insider', particularly in highly communal societies. As Schutte has asserted, 'unless exceptional measures are taken to promote a good dialogue', it is extremely difficult to have a non-hierarchical dialogue.[60] Schuttee refers to this as 'incommeasurability' based on an

---

[57]Groundhog day, also called *Jour de la Marmotte*, is a traditional holiday celebrated on 2 February to welcome spring. The phrase is colloquially associated with repetitive patterns and events that are difficult to avoid.

[58]Catherine Barnes, *Renegotiating the Political Settlement in War-to-peace Transitions* (London: Conciliation Resources, 2009), 3–4.

[59]Marnia Lazreg, 'Development: Feminist Theory's Cul-de-Sac', in *Feminist Post-development Thought: Rethinking Modernity, Post-colonialism and Representation*, ed. Kriemild Saunders (London: Zed Books, 2002), 125.

[60]Ofelia Schutte, 'Cultural Alterity: Cross-cultural Communication and Feminist Theory in North–South Contexts', *Hypatia* 13 (1998): 56.

analysis located in relations between dominant and subaltern people across borders.[61] This non-hierarchical dialogue is one of the most transformative pieces on the chess table in conflicted societies, but it is profoundly difficult to move effectively. Not least it requires a commitment to relationship building, mutual trust, keeping promises and ultimately being prepared to take time to do the work. This language affirms a differently articulated set of priorities, a distinct move from the power of the gun to dictate the when and how of the negotiation process. The dynamics of political settlement have invariably functioned on a time axis that gives little credence to this slow coalition and relationship-building exercise, and its inclusion would fundamentally reorder and slow down how we do the business of negotiation. As the Feminist of Color Collective notes in its reflection on bargaining across political borders and colonial pasts, 'political solidarity depends on a careful negotiation of difference'.[62] That difference is not only visible in how the talking is done, but in the time it takes to do it.

Conclusion

How does one distinguish between the continuation of the status quo through other means and transformation in political settlement? What kind of markers might be engaged to achieve structural and deep-seated change for women? What theory of change supports transformation for women and how do we avoid bureaucratic and technocratic theories of change that merely reproduce the status quo for women in society? The limited existing literature identifies the following factors as essential in addressing women's role within political settlements:

> [E]lite support for a gender equity agenda; [the] ability of the women's movement to contain oppositional elite or non elite groups; transnational discourse and actors creating space for the gender equity agenda; presence of male allies and 'femocrats' within the state apparatus; and policy coalitions exerting pressure on the state.[63]

Beyond those concrete suggestions, this article has suggested that some further work needs to be done. Specifically, an essential move mandates 'critical friendship' with and moderate distance from elites. Without some recalibration and interrogation of the gendered construction of elite positioning to account for historical race and gender edifices of privilege, the likelihood of fundamental changes to political settlement practices is small. This move is not merely valuable for cosmetic purposes but progresses from a recognition that the legitimacy of settlement processes embedded without primary integration of women in process and outcome is low. This analysis demonstrates that when one hooks the critical tools of feminist analysis into political settlement practice, the legitimacy quota of this analytical tool further diminishes. Such forensic review leaves little scope for comfort to those who advance political settlement as the intellectual and policy panacea for the multiple ills of violent, fragile and exclusionary societies. Rather, it should prompt some essential rethinking, with a view to harnessing the transformative potential of gender-directed review to generating better political outcomes for fragile and conflict-affected states.

---

[61]Ibid.

[62]The Santa Cruz Feminist of Color Collective, 'Building on 'The Edge of Each Other's Battles": A Feminist of Color Multidimensional Lens', *Hypatia* 29 (2014): 30.

[63]Sohela Nazneen and Simeen Mahmud, 'Gendered Politics of Securing Inclusive Development' (working paper, Effective States and Inclusive Development Research Centre, The University of Manchester, 2012), 3.

There is further need to frame the existing political opportunity structure for women in specific place, culture and history and contextualise the opportunities for women's engagement in the local. So, probing political settlement requires not only a broad engagement with key macro politics, but must remain attuned to the specific experiences and exclusion women experience in micro political settings. Contextual analysis attuned to cultural and social conditions is critical. Beyond the formal institutional entry points for women, accounting for the expansive influence of informal relations on women's capacity to engage in and be influential in political processes is essential to linking the public and private domains. The importance of informal relationships is linked to another central plank to a new approach, namely: the relationship between public and private ordering for women, and the extent to which insecurity and under-enforcement in the private realm have a barrier effect for women's entry into the public arena.

In conclusion, the fundamental question is whether political settlement analysis can have its parameters expanded and incorporate (gender) ideology, (gender) discourses, bottom-up strategies used in negotiations by non-elite actors and informal interactions.[64] Its ability to do so may well inform and enable its ambition to provide transformative capacity to tenuous political spaces and the women and men who inhabit them.

Acknowledgements

Thanks to Professor Christine Bell and Eilish Rooney for comments on earlier drafts of this work and to Griffin Ferry for research assistance.

Disclosure statement

No potential conflict of interest was reported by the author.

Funding

The work was supported by the Department for International Development, UK Government [grant number PO 6663].

---

[64]Adapted from Sohela Nazneen and Simeen Mahmud, 'Gendered Politics of Securing Inclusive Development'.

Light, heat and shadows: women's reflections on peacebuilding in post-conflict Bougainville

Nicole George

School of Political Science and International Studies, University of Queensland, Brisbane, Australia

ABSTRACT
In this paper, I examine women's reflections on their experiences as peacebuilders during Bougainville's long years of conflict and the later period of conflict transition. I discuss the varying ways in which women, in this predominantly matrilineal society, recounted their contributions to conflict resolution as part of broader efforts to build peace. My interlocutors told stories of the distinctiveness of women's peace leadership, interwoven with references to global policy frameworks such as United Nations Security Council Resolution 1325. This appears, at first glance, to evidence a positive story of global and local influences coming together to produce positive peacebuilding outcomes charged by 'light and heat', as theorised by Annika Björkdahl and Kristine Höglund. I show this story to also be one of shadows, however, arguing that deeper scrutiny of these perspectives on women's peace leadership suggest they also mask difficult and more complex local realities.

How do interrelated global and local influences shape women's experiences of, and reflections on, peacebuilding? This question has assumed increased urgency in the last decades as specialists in peacebuilding and development investigate the benefits of developing less externally driven, and more people-centred and participatory, approaches to their programmes so that they better reflect local expectations, aspirations and values.[1] When confronting this so-called 'local turn' in peacebuilding and development from a feminist perspective however, we find evidence which affirms *and* disputes its utility. Feminist scrutiny of localised socio-political contexts might draw attention to the way women activists challenge gender discrimination and women's marginalisation, and in this process, reference cultural and religious values which advocate the respectful and equal treatment of women, or legitimate their participation as leaders in their communities.[2]

---

[1] Roger Mac Ginty and Oliver Richmond, 'The Fallacy of Constructing Hybrid Political Orders: A Reappraisal of the Hybrid Turn in Peacebuilding', *International Peacekeeping* (November 5, 2015), http://dx.doi.org/10.1080/13533312.2015.1099440 ; and Deborah Eade, Capacity Building: An Approach to People Centered Development (Oxford: Oxfam, 2005).

[2] Nicole George, 'Starting with a Prayer: Women, Faith, and Security in Fiji', Oceania 85, no. 1 (2015): 119–31; Nicole George, "Just like your mother?' The Politics of Feminism and Maternity in the Pacifi c Islands', *The Australian Feminist Law Journal* 32 (2010): 77–96; and Sally Engle Merry, 'Transnational Human Rights and Local Activism: Mapping The Middle', *American Anthropologist* 108, no. 1 (2006): 38–51.

But the pioneering work conducted by Annika Björkdahl, with co-authors Christina Höglund and Anna Selimovic, also makes clear the gendered challenges of this effort to work more closely between 'bottom-up' and 'top-down' sites of conflict transition.[3] Drawing on Anna Tsing's foundational research on globalisation and friction,[4] Björkdahl, and her co-authors have emphasised the 'frictions' that occur when there is an interplay between global and local influences and the extent to which 'power relations' and 'local agency' working in cooperation with more formalised sites of authority can be generative of their own gendered exclusions.[5] Hence, they draw attention to the fact that the specific forms of social order that are legitimated in such contexts may not create improved outcomes for all and may be particularly restrictive for women, constraining their participation and visibility to only those domains that are deemed 'acceptable' or 'appropriate'.[6]

It is this contention that frames my exploration of women's peacebuilding in Bougainville, a mineral-rich Pacific Island territory of Papua New Guinea which experienced 10 years of secessionist warfare erupting in the 1980s and where today, peace has a fragile quality. Estimates of the loss of life in this conflict vary, with the most serious suggesting between 5 and 10% of the territory's population killed and one-third displaced.[7] Women played key roles in the early stages of the conflict within the rebel secessionist movement. In later stages as the conflict became more protracted, they acted as influential peacebuilders. In both capacities they drew on Bougainville's matrilineal traditions and authority structures to legitimise this activity.

Since 2000, women leaders have invoked the international Women, Peace and Security agenda (WPS), as established in United Nations Security Council Resolution (UNSCR) 1325 and subsequent related resolutions, to promote women's participation in Bougainville's long process of conflict transition.[8] This global–local discourse places a heavy emphasis upon women's successes as peace negotiators during the conflict and the importance of understanding the continued contributions women can make as peace leaders. As I will demonstrate, these recollections tend to emphasise the gender-appropriate nature of this activity and how it is supported by matrilineal cultural, as well as faith-based, protocols emphasising gendered duty and virtue. This has prompted me to consider where and how this type of rhetoric obscures other more complex aspects of women's leadership in conflict, as well as the violence some women endured as peace leaders.

In the following sections of this article, I develop these ideas more fully. My discussion draws from second-hand sources, development agencies' grey literature on the conflict, and principally, from first-hand testimony collected through 20 long-duration interviews conducted in June 2014 in Bougainville, with women leaders active in church, community,

---

[3]Annika Björkdahl, 'A Gender-just Peace? Exploring the Post-Dayton Peace Process', *Global Peace and Change* 37, no. 2 (2012): 286–317; Björkdahl, Annika and Kristine Höglund, 'Precarious Peacebuilding: Friction in Global/Local Encounters', *Peacebuilding* 1, no. 3 (2013): 292; and Björkdahl Annika and Johanna Mannegren Selimovic, 'Gendering Agency in Transitional Justice', *Security Dialogue* 46, no. 2 (2015): 165–82.

[4]See note 1 above.

[5]Björkdahl and Selimovic, 'Gendering Agency', 167.

[6]Björkdahl, 'A Gender-just Peace'.

[7]John Braithwaite, 'Rape Shame and Pride' (address to Stockholm Criminology Symposium, June 16, 2006), https://www.anu.edu.au/fellows/jbraithwaite/_documents/Stockholm_Prise_Address.pdf (accessed September 17, 2015).

[8]Sharon Bhagwan Rolls, 'Pacific Regional Perspectives on Women and the Media: Making the Connection with UN Security Council Resolution 1325 (Women Peace and Security) and Section J of the Beijing Platform for Action', *Signs* 36, no. 3 (2012): 570–77.

political and economic domains. On the one hand, evidence from these sources seems to support a positive story of global and local influences coming together to produce positive frictional outcomes for women peacebuilders charged by 'light and heat'.[9] On the other hand, I show these 'positive' outcomes to be accompanied by shadows in the form of leadership activity that is unrecognised and silences on certain gendered aspects of women's conflict activity that persist. My contention is that these interleaving global and local discourses come together in ways that form a highly feminised, and perhaps fetishized, portrait of women's agency as peacebuilders. This portrait may not necessarily be empowering in the longer term and may mask other more complex gendered experiences of conflict.

This discussion proceeds in three parts. I first develop the conceptual and theoretical framework which guides my discussion, explaining the value of the 'friction' concept as an analytical device to support my examination of narratives of women's peacebuilding. In the following section, I give some brief history to the conflict in Bougainville and explain where and how women have been visible in the crisis and in the later context of post-conflict governance. In the final section of this discussion, I draw from my own interview-based work in Bougainville to examine where and how women's references to their peacebuilding reflects both global and local influences and how these are, at once, enabling and constraining.

Gender, friction and peacebuilding

In sync (although perhaps not always in dialogue) with broader peace and conflict research investigating participatory and people-centred approaches to conflict mediation, is the considerable body of feminist research on women's peacebuilding. This work has demonstrated the impact and influence of women's 'resilient' everyday responses to conflict, and their positive contributions to localised 'bottom-up' peacebuilding processes.[10] It has often also offered a simultaneous critique of top-down, institutionalised efforts to mediate conflict, showing how these are prone to ignore women's local agency, or to include women, but only insofar as they conform to a gendered script that requires them to be 'passive, civilian and protected'.[11]

Feminist peace and conflict research has also complicated the portrait of 'bottom-up' and participatory approaches to peace however. For example, this research has identified the constraints for women, and for peace itself, when local leaders draw on gendered constructs to harden the divisions and disgruntlements that fuel violent conflict and win support for their belligerent ambitions. Appeals to masculinised norms of honour and courage are frequently voiced in such contexts, encouraging citizens to equate the protection of 'helpless women and children' with protection of 'the nation'.[12]

This rhetoric emphasises vigilance to the threats posed to communities from outside. Yet, it often also means that women within the community itself become objects of surveillance and punished for acts of gender dissidence, that is, acts which flout norms of

---

[9]Björkdahl and Höglund, 'Precarious Peacebuilding', 292.

[10]Malathi de Alwis, Julie Mertus, and Tazreena Sajjad, 'Women and Peace Processes', in *Women and Wars*, ed. Carol Cohn (Cambridge: Polity, 2013), 169–93.

[11]Björkdahl 'A Gender-Just Peace', 288, 291.

[12]Carol Cohn, 'Women and Wars: Toward a Conceptual Framework', in *Women and Wars,* ed. C. Cohn (Cambridge: Polity, 2013), 1; and Iris Marion Young, 'The Logic of Masculinist Protection: Reflections on the Current Security State', *Signs* 29, no. 1 (2003): 1–25.

gender-appropriate behaviour.[13] In such contexts, women who resist conflict may be viewed as disloyal or unpatriotic because their ambitions are judged harmful to the community's broader security.[14] Alternatively, there may be an expectation that women advocate for peace in highly gendered and localised terms, legitimising their opposition to conflict by showing how it obstructs, or makes more difficult, their capacities as dutiful mothers, wives or daughters. This may be political enabling at one level,[15] but it may also make it hard for women peace activists to build broader public political roles in ways that extend beyond their capacities as dutiful carers.

Globally, women's networks have worked to raise awareness of how local and global forces come together to jeopardise the security of women in conflict and restrict the work of women peacebuilders. In 2000, their lobbying and advocacy work delivered a positive policy outcome when the United National Security Council passed Resolution 1325. This resolution focused international policy-makers' attention on the gendered impacts of conflict and the particular difficulties experienced by women in contexts riven by war and violence. It also affirmed 'the important role of women in the prevention and resolution of conflicts and in peace-building' and asserted women's right to 'equal participation and full involvement in all efforts for the maintenance and promotion of peace and security' (UNSC 2000).[16]

Even while formal implementation of the WPS agenda within state policy remains slow,[17] this policy framework provides women peace activists with powerful tools for lobbying. In the Pacific Islands region the WPS agenda is described as a 'loud hailer' which enables women to draw national, regional and international attention to the achievements they have made as peacebuilders and to demand higher levels of participation in debates on regional and national security.[18] But in the light of the earlier discussion focused on the way conflict can create a restrictive environment for women, and constrain their peacebuilding ambitions, it is important to enquire as to how the WPS framework is re-articulated and framed in localised contexts and as activists respond to the bottom-up influences and pressures of the local political environment. Does the effort to align women's local peace activism with the global WPS agenda allow women to realise new opportunities as peacebuilders? Is the movement between global and local frames perhaps more partial and selective?

Björkdahl and Höglund's use of 'friction' is useful for investigating these dynamics. I draw upon it here to critically question how women's 'local' experience of conflict and peacebuilding is (re)constituted when it is articulated in dialogue with the women, peace and security policy discourse. The concept of friction draws attention to the production of 'new power dynamics' created as a result of 'the fragmentary intersection of ideas and norms in the global/local conversation'.[19] Borrowing from Anna Tsing's foundational work

---

[13]Carol Cohn and Ruth Jacobson, 'Women and Political Activism in the Face of War and Militarization', in *Women and Wars*, ed. C. Cohn (Cambridge: Polity, 2013), 102–23; Malathi de Alwis, Julie Mertus, and Tazreena Sajjad, 'Women and Peace Processes', 178; and Björkdahl and Selimovic, 'Gendering Agency in Transitional Justice', 167.

[14]Laura McLeod, 'A Feminist Approach to Hybridity: Understanding Local and International Interactions in Producing Post-Conflict Gender Security', *Journal of Intervention and Statebuilding* 9, no. 1 (2015): 54.

[15]George, 'Starting with a Prayer'; and George, 'Just Like your Mother'.

[16]United Nations Security Council, *United Nations Security Council Resolution 1325* (New York: United Nations, 2000), http://daccess-ods.un.org/TMP/4847382.90309906.html (accessed March 22, 2010).

[17]Nicole Pratt and Sophie Richter-Devroe, 'Critically Examining UNSCR 1325 on Women, Peace and Security', *International Feminist Journal of Politics* 13 no. 4 (2011): 492.

[18]FemLINK Pacific, 'Women, Peace and Security: Policy Brief on UN Security Council Resolution 1325', no. 1, http://www.femlinkpacific.org.fj/images/PDF/Policy/FemLINKPACIFIC_WPS1325_Policybrief1.pdf.

[19]See note 9 above.

on friction as a metaphor to capture the complex interplay and reconfiguration that occurs in global and local encounters,[20] Björkdahl and Höglund use this term to examine how 'global ideas pertaining to liberal peace are charged and changed by their encounters with post-conflict realities'.[21] 'Two sticks rubbed together create light and heat' they contend, 'alone they are just sticks'.[22] In her elaboration on this theme, Björkdahl draws attention to the frictional processes and agency of peace localisers (non-government organisations, peace activists, religious leaders and individuals) who take 'ideas and norms' prevailing in global policy discourse on peace and security and attempt to 'reframe them … in terms that are acceptable in the local context'.[23] This perspective indicates the importance of investigating the frictional light and heat that may be produced when local women reflect on their experiences of conflict through the WPS lens. But we are required to consider the shadows that are cast by this process too. In the following sections of this article, I develop this analysis in more detail. I begin, this discussion, however, with some brief background on the conflict in Bougainville and women's experiences of this crisis.

Gender and conflict in Bougainville

Many Bougainvilleans hold secessionist ambitions and question the incorporation of their islands first, into the Australian protectorate of New Guinea, and later, the independent state of Papua New Guinea (PNG).[24] These separatist grievances were sharpened in the 1960s when the Australian-owned mining enterprise Conzinc Rio Tinto Australia (CRA) established a large open cut copper mine on Bougainville's main island. In the post-independence context, the mine, one of the largest and richest open-cut enterprises in the world, was a considerable export revenue earner for the PNG government. Locally, however, it remained a source of resentment for those living in its vicinity; they saw it as an imposition and a threat to the environment. Local resentments were also generated by the mine workforce, mainly expatriates or PNG nationals, who were perceived as disrespectful of Bougainvillean custom. These feelings escalated in 1988 when a Bougainvillean nurse was raped by mainland mine workers.[25] The idea that Bougainvillean women required protection from this 'foreign' workforce became a motivation for some rebellious activity, inspiring fighters to resist threats posed by 'outsiders … raping and terrorising our women'.[26]

A local campaign of sabotage carried out against mine infrastructure began to intensify from this time onwards. The PNG government, eager to protect the mine's lucrative income sent security forces to protect the mine site. This was a blunt incursion that resulted in local casualties and escalated tensions. An intensification of the conflict followed with a more organised force of home-grown separatists (some of them former PNG Defence force personnel) fighting against Papua New Guinea military forces (assisted with Australian

---

[20]Tsing, Friction.

[21]See note 9 above.

[22]Ibid.

[23]Björkdahl 2012, 293.

[24]John Braithwaite et al., *Reconciliation and Architectures of Commitment: Sequencing Peace in Bougainville* (Canberra: ANU Press, 2010); Regan Anthony, 'Development and Conflict: The Struggle for Self-determination in Bougainville', in *Security and Development in the Pacific Islands: Social Resilience in Emerging States,* ed. Anne M. Brown (Boulder: Lynne Reiner, 2010).

[25]Sam Kauona cited in Braithwaite et al., *Architectures of Commitment,* 114.

[26]Sam Kauona, 'Freedom from Fear', in *Peace on Bougainville: Truce Monitoring Group Gudpel Nius Bilong Peace,* ed. Rebecca Adams (Wellington: Victoria University Press, 2001), 85.

military hardware and logistical support).[27] By the end of the conflict, the lines were blurred and Bougainvilleans were warring amongst themselves, 'brother against brother' as it is locally explained.[28] Populations fled to the bush to escape the fighting, infrastructure was destroyed. A blockade imposed on the islands by the PNG government, designed to halt the importation of arms and munitions, also deprived populations of food, medicines and consumable goods. Bougainvilleans displayed great resourcefulness during this period, but this was amidst great suffering.[29]

Women as conflict protagonists

Women's capacities as peace-brokers are typically the most celebrated aspect of women's experience of the conflict but this story has obscured the roles women played in resistance to the mine and later within the secessionist camp. As early as 1969, the Australian Minister for Commonwealth Territories, Charles Barnes, toured the region and was confronted by a troupe of Nasioi women who sang about their sacred connections to the land and their inability to understand why it was no longer theirs.[30] In later years, women were also involved in more confrontational protests, throwing themselves bare-breasted in traditional dress in front of the mine's bulldozers. This opposition was confronted with state force but it never petered out, despite hopeful predictions from mine advisors that it would.[31]

By the 1980s, when unrest surfaced again, women were still centrally involved. At this time a local woman, Perpetua Serero (Bougainville's first female radio announcer) and her cousin, Francis Ona, led a new landowners association that was opposed to mine and by 1988 was carrying out sophisticated campaigns of industrial sabotage.[32] Hilary Charlesworth also notes how, in a later period at the height of the conflict, women were involved in a massacre of PNG Defence Forces at Kangu Beach, encouraging them to put down their arms and play volleyball, and leading them into an ambush planned by Bougainville Revolutionary Army (BRA) personnel that left 12 dead and more wounded.[33]

Women as peace protagonists

As the conflict raged on and became more chaotic, so its civilian and gendered costs became more pronounced. And women's questioning of the conflict became more acute. Cultural and religious structures which established women's matrilineal authority over land and in decision-making in many (although not all) parts of the country, were certainly undermined in initial negotiations at the mine site and as a consequence of the mass importation of mine labour from the PNG mainland and Australia. But the impacts of the conflict itself saw a further diminution of these values. As one local woman leader explained, 'the gun

---

[27]Braithwaite et al., *Architectures of Commitment*.
[28]Local women's representative (1), Interview with Author, June 18, 2014.
[29]Amnesty International (Bougainville: The Forgotten Human Rights Tragedy, 1997), https://www.amnesty.org/download/Documents/160000/asa340011997en.pdf (accessed September 18, 2015).
[30]Braithwaite et al., *Architectures of Commitment*, 15.
[31]Braithwaite et al., *Architectures of Commitment*, 15–18.
[32]Kristian Laslett, 'State Crime by Proxy', *British Journal of Criminology* 52, no. 3 (2012): 708.
[33]Charlesworth, 'Are Women Peaceful', 353.

was the new power'[34]; in this context women were exposed to high levels of conflict related violence and abuse including rape.[35]

Experiences of deprivation, fear and conflict-related violence were not borne without resistance however and prompted women in Bougainville to challenge their predicament and reassert their matrilineal authority. This involved women reaching out across the country, through their church networks, to send messages of peace, or 'peace-baskets' of scarce items to one another.[36] Although movement around the islands was restricted, women also succeeded in arranging national meetings so that they could share their perspectives on the conflict. As one woman peace leader explained it, when women met, they realised that although they may have had different political views and supported different actors, they were not 'enemies'.[37] Indeed concerns for their children, their families and the future of their country were mutually held across the lines of the conflict and united women.

This focus on motherhood was used frequently to legitimate women's calls for peace, and saw women refer to their matrilineal cultural roles which stipulated that they were 'mothers of the land' with a sacred obligation to protect Bougainville and its people from further violence.[38] This matrilineal authority extended to all women. Explaining why he chose to participate in the 1994 Arawa Peace conference, one BRA platoon leader put it this way: '[i]n our culture, you are supposed to listen to your sister. If she gives you advice, you are supposed to take it'.[39]

The idea that there was a sacred dimension to women's peacebuilding capacities was also enhanced by the Marian traditions of Catholic faith that are followed by most Bougainvilleans. As Anna Karina Hermkens has shown, Mary's attributes of peacefulness are entangled with customary representations of Bougainvillean motherhood. Women peacebuilders, therefore claimed that 'Mama Maria' gave them the strength to promote peace, would protect them as they stood between lines of fighting, and lent persuasive weight to appeals that combatants lay down their arms.[40]

Building on their work as 'bottom-up' peacebuilders,[41] women were involved in many of the formal peace negotiations that occurred during the conflict. These were locally organised in Arawa, on Bougainville in 1994, but took a more concentrated and internationally supported form in Burnham and Lincoln in New Zealand in the late 1990s and built towards the 1998 Arawa Truce Agreement that declared a permanent ceasefire. The final Comprehensive Peace Agreement was established in 2001 and saw Bougainville declared an autonomous territory of PNG.[42]

As the peace process gathered momentum, transitional governments took various forms and women were given representation in these administrations. Three women also sat on the 24-member Constitutional Commission that deliberated on the future structures of

---

[34]Local woman's representative (1) in conversation with author, Buka June 18, 2014.
[35]Braithwaite, 'Rape, Shame and Pride'.
[36]Ibid.
[37]Local woman's representative (2) in conversation with author, Buka June 17, 2014.
[38]Josephine Sirivi and Marylin. T. Havini, *As Mothers of the Land: The Birth of the Bougainville Women for Peace and Freedom* (Canberra: Pandanus Books, 2004); Anna-Karina Hermkens, 'Mary, Motherhood and Nation: Religion and Gender Ideology in Bougainville's Secessionist warfare', *Intersections: Gender and Sexuality in Asia and the Pacific* 25 Feb, http://intersections.anu.edu.au/issue25/hermkens.htm, (accessed September 13, 2014).
[39]Cited Braithwaite et al., *Architectures of Commitment*, 116.
[40]Hermkens, 'Mary, Motherhood and Nation'.
[41]Braithwaite et al., *Architectures of Commitment*, 1.
[42]Ibid., 35–49.

institutional governance for the autonomous territory between 2002 and 2004. In recognition of their contributions to peace and their matrilineal customary standing, women were also granted three reserved seats in Bougainville's 39-seat territorial parliament.

A considerable international aid presence has followed on the heels of the peace processes, with Australian and New Zealand governments the largest contributors to Bougainville's post-conflict recovery.[43] Their programmes include funding support for peacebuilding initiatives, social welfare programmes and public infrastructure development schemes. Local women's non-government organisations such as the Leitana Nehan Women's Development Agency (LNWDA), the Nazareth Rehabilitation Centre and the Bougainville Women's Federation have also been the key beneficiaries of these development programmes.[44]

Gender and friction on Bougainville

As I have shown, women played important leadership roles as tensions escalated on Bougainville, contributing to the resistance movement that built around the Panguna mine, and as active collaborators and supporters in some aspects of combat. At a later point, women also played a significant role in building bottom-up momentum for peace on Bougainville and they continue to contribute to conflict transformation to this day. This work is continued by women peace leaders such as the Sister Lorraine Garusu, and Josephine Sirivi who, sometimes independently and sometimes with the support of the aid agencies mentioned above, have developed community-based programmes to assist the reintegration of ex-combatants, and to meet the needs of the generation of young people whose lives and education were disrupted by the crisis.[45]

Women in Bougainville, as elsewhere in the Pacific, have also have looked to UNSCR 1325 to reinforce the value of their bottom-up peace campaigns. In the years since the signing of the Bougainville Peace Agreement in 2000, the international language of the WPS framework has been invoked as part of efforts to ensure that women's peace work will not be forgotten and to promote women's rights to participate in all aspects of the conflict transition process. In this regard, noted local peace activist Helen Hakena from LNWDA has developed awareness-raising programmes on UNSCR 1325 which she describes as a 'very precious' and valuable resource to assist women's 'participation in their local level government'. [46] At the government level, former minister for women in the Bougainville Autonomous Government, Rose Pihei, also developed a draft National Action Plan on Women Peace and Security for Bougainville but this is yet to be formally institutionalised.

In my own personal interactions and discussions with women leaders on Bougainville, I found that references to the global WPS policy frameworks were interleaved with references to the local customary frameworks that endowed women's peace advocacy with legitimacy. Almost universally, my interlocutors were keen for me to understand that 'women brought peace to this country' and repeated this refrain many times in our interviews. In recounting this history, women's testimonies frequently pivoted on ideas about maternal responsibility

---

[43] Jonathon Makuwira, 'Aid Partnership in Bougainville: The Case of a Local Women's NGO and its Donors', *Development in Practice* 16, no. 3–4 (2006): 322–33.

[44] Ibid.

[45] This work was explained to me in interviews conducted with Sirivi in Arawa on June 24, 2014, and with Garasu in Chabbai on June 22.

[46] Hakena, Helen cited FemLINK PACIFIC, *Policy Brief on UN Security Council Resolution 1325*.

BUILDING PEACE

and how this shaped women's distinctive responses to conflict related danger as being more considered and thoughtful than men's fight or flee response. My interlocutors also explained the matrilineal, customary and religious influences that shaped their peacebuilding work. On this latter point, they seemed keen to explain how women's peacebuilding work adhered to feminised, and in some instances, sacred ideals establishing a rightful path of peace advocacy according to gendered norms established in faith and culture.

Constructing the peacebuilding fetish: 'She makes war, she makes peace'

There were, however, troubling aspects to this narrative. When I asked about the challenges that women negotiate in promoting this discourse of peacebuilding, rooted in the local and given enhanced legitimacy by the global (that is UNSCR 1325), respondents frequently discussed a 'lack of capacity' as a major barrier to improve their limited access to decision-making opportunities. Further enquiry about what form the capacity problem took, prompted many women to identify leadership as a key challenge. One woman member of parliament explained her concerns about a lack of leadership capacity in the following way:

> Women have to come together, other women don't want to share leadership. But we are not thinking together … we need to bring the village women up because women many times look down on themselves.[47]

Another women leader explained the challenge similarly:

> We need to build capacity in women's leadership. In church organisations. Women need to come up … women are not educated enough to take leadership roles … we need to mould new leaders.[48]

For another local observer, the 'problem' of capacity, was expressed in a way that linked leadership, influence and women's matrilineal values when she stated:

> We need to educate women to know their roles and responsibilities as mothers – in the family, at the local level, at the community, regional and national level … but women don't have the power to influence for lack of knowledge. They need to understand more about issues.[49]

It is not unusual for women leaders in the Pacific region to speak of capacity as a problem. But in this context, where women had played such a well-recognised roles in the conflict, these reflections also seemed ironic. As I recorded them, I reflected on the contrasts they established with accounts of the conflict period and the well-documented resourcefulness and leadership women had demonstrated during the crisis as conflict protagonists and as peacebuilders. Why, in a period of greater stability, with more robust international policy resources such as UNSCR 1325, and more aid assistance, did women leaders now express a lack of confidence in their capacities? In particular, I was puzzled by their suggestion that their place in the familial, village and maternal realm, as well as within church networks, impeded their understanding and capacity to act, indeed lead, on broader issues.

To ponder this is not to deny the significant challenges that women have faced in the period since Bougainville's crisis abated. A peace-audit conducted by Bougainville's Department of Veterans Affairs in 2008–2010 found that for many people, the post-conflict

---

[47]Parliamentary representative (1), interview with author, Buka, June 20, 2014.
[48]Coordinator, Women's NGO, interview with author, Buka, June 20, 2014.
[49]Parliamentary representative (2), interview with author, Buka, June 17, 2014.

years have been ones marked by a lack of opportunity, resentment and frustration.[50] These tendencies are amplified amongst ex-combatants and the country's youth, few of whom have had access to higher education or employment opportunities.[51] In this climate, the auditors found that a logic of force had replaced older values such as respect for elders, chiefs or women's matrilineal authority and the customary roles these groups play in the non-violent resolution of disputes. They also noted a rise in women's insecurity that was said to go against 'the matrilineal grain of Bougainville society'.[52] These factors were, therefore, all identified in the final audit report as contributing to a 'diminution of women's peacebuilding role' in the post-conflict context.[53]

Even so, each time I heard the word 'capacity' raised by my interlocutors I could not help but reflect on the considerable development aid industry presence on Bougainville and the likelihood that these conversations were inflected by the globally pervasive 'capacity-building' development paradigm.[54] Like the local turn in peacebuilding (see earlier sections of this article), this approach to participatory and people-centred development emphasises increased recognition of local people's aspirations and values.[55] However as Deborah Eade has shown, these programmes can invariably be delivered in a fashion that ignores, misunderstands or diminishes the very local capacities that they are designed to promote.[56]

Capacity-building programmes conducted on the WPS agenda with Bougainville's women (often funded by the Australian government and undertaken through intermediary and local women's NGOs in the region),[57] seem on the one hand to have encouraged women to reconstitute their experiences as rightful and dutiful agents of 'bottom-up' peacebuilding. On the other hand, they have discouraged recognition of women's contributions to the secessionist movement during the conflict. As I have shown, in this capacity too, women's authority to act and to lead was understood to be legitimate (at least at the time), garnered following from within clans and villages, and was enabled by the dutiful or sacred roles women held as mothers and sources of matrilineal authority. Josephine Sirivi made this point plainly to me as she responded to my questions regarding women's customary roles in conflict. The woman is the 'strength of the clan' she explained. 'She makes war, she makes peace.'[58]

Yet when appraised through the WPS lens in Bougainville, the narrative focus is rather more selectively placed on the 'she makes peace' story of women's experiences of conflict as the one which generates light and heat. These discourses make a gendered virtue of women's peacebuilding but do not emphasise its political content. Indeed, the particularly feminised reconstitution of women's peacebuilding capacities, and the repeated mentions of women's maternal and faith-based responsibilities as motivations for this activity, seems to have emptied it of any political content. On occasion, women's peacebuilding was described by

---

[50]Department of Veterans Affairs, (Autonomous Region of Bougainville) and AusAID Democratic Governance Project, *Bougainville Peacebuilding Project Report*, (Buka: DVA and AusAID, 2010), October 3.

[51]Ibid.

[52]Ibid., 77.

[53]Ibid.

[54]Jonathon Makuwira, 'Aid Partnership in the Bougainville Conflict'.

[55]Deborah Eade, *Capacity Building: An Approach to People Centered Development* (Oxford: Oxfam, 2005).

[56]Ibid., 3.

[57]FemLINK PACIFIC, *Peace Talks: Promoting United Nations Resolution Women, Peace and Security in the Pacific* (2012), http://www.femlinkpacific.org.fj/_resources/main/images/uploads/Promoting_UNSCR1325_in_the_Pacific_region.pdf.

[58]Sirivi, interview with author, Arawa, June 24, 2014.

my interlocutors almost as inherent feminine *reflex* to conflict and instability rather than a skilled intervention. Perhaps, it was this depoliticised and frictional framing of women's conflict leadership that prompted participants in my research to lament the deficits of women's leadership in the post-conflict context and the inability of women in village and church networks and as mothers, to understand and respond to present challenges and 'issues'.

Certainly, Bougainvillean women's limited success in the post-conflict electoral domain, and particularly their difficulty in winning parliamentary representation beyond Bougainville's three reserved seats,[59] suggest that this frictional narrative of women's leadership in conflict has not helped women's longer term political ambitions. Shining more light onto the capacities that women displayed as critical contributors to, and, in some instances, instigators of the rebel secessionist movement, may be an uncomfortable disruption to the light and heat narrative of women and peace as it is articulated amongst women in Bougainville. But re-emphasising these capacities may also increase the electorate's awareness of women's political acumen. Without acknowledging this more politicised role in conflict, women's peacebuilding seems to resemble a feminised fetish. Making a virtue of women's pacifist customary and maternal roles may be empowering in localised village, clan and parish domains, but women leaders also seemed frustrated that this feminised representation of women's leadership has not provided a secure foundation from to build the broader forms of national political credibility that will make women electable

Shadows cast by the peacebuilding fetish

The continued focus on the 'she makes peace' aspect of women's conflict involvement has also diverted attention away from some of the darker experiences that have accompanied women's peacebuilding activity. These became evident to me in the shadowy recollections of violence that my informants shared when they discussed their experiences as peace activists. I use the term shadowy, because although this testimony was often a fleeting presence in my interviews, it prompted me to critically reflect on the risks that may accompany women's contributions to peacebuilding.[60] It often began with my informants describing the mistrust and suspicion that greeted their peacebuilding efforts. In contexts where the 'gun was the new law'[61] and force competed with custom as sources of authority, women's efforts to speak about peace with combatants were not always received respectfully and frequently made them targets of suspicion and allegations of 'enemy' collaboration.

Some of my informants quietly described how these allegations resulted in them being subjected to 'torture'. While they did not seem comfortable lingering on this subject, and I did not feel comfortable probing for more detail, these stories were recounted with enough frequency for me to understand that this violence was an experience that was shared by many women active in the effort to reconcile combatants and build peace. It was recounted to me by women located in various parts of the country and by women with different political affiliations, by women who had lived with their dependants in bush camps, and

---

[59]Kerryn Baker, *Pawa Blong Meri: Women Candidates in the 2015 Bougainville Election* (SSGM Discussion Paper, 2015/14, no. 6), http://ips.cap.anu.edu.au/sites/default/files/DP-2015-14-Baker-ONLINE.pdf.

[60]This information will not be attributed directly to my informants to protect anonymity and personal safety. Correlation of these testimonies is found in reports produced by Amnesty International during the crisis period (see note 31), and in the findings of the Peace Audit conducted in Bougainville in 2010 (see note 52).

[61]Woman peace leader in interview with author, June 18, 2014.

by women who had sought shelter in the 'care centres' policed by the PNGDF personnel. Even women's humanitarian efforts were subject to this kind of response as I learnt when one of my interlocutors described the violent beating she suffered at the hands of a care centre guard as she pleaded for the centre authorities to provide medical assistance to save the life of a severely ill child. The camp authorities were suspicious because the child came from a resistance-controlled area.

Here again the frictional narrative of women's peacebuilding seemed to cast shadows. Efforts to frame this activity in ways which emphasised its resonance with maternal and sacred responsibilities established in custom and in Christian faith were usually positively focused on the light and heat (successes and influence) of this activity. Hence, the story of women's peacebuilding in Bougainville is one which emphasises women's agency in conflict, not their victimhood and certainly not the idea that women's peacebuilding agency could also expose them to violence. These more troubling testimonies suggested that women's peacebuilding was not understood universally in the local context as an uncontested virtue. It certainly did not make women immune to the violence and divisions that consumed the territory and often put them in situations of profound risk. In the post-conflict context, these scenarios were recalled by one of my informants as Bougainville's 'untold story'. [62]

This says something critical about the gendered quality of peace on Bougainville and women's role in its construction. Women may have 'brought peace to Bougainville', as my interlocutors were so quick to remind me, but it is not a peace that enables deliberations on this kind of gendered violence. This is particularly important given that initial conflict was fuelled, at least in part as an action to protect the territory's women. [63] If women peacebuilders, themselves, seem disinclined to discuss their exposure to this violence, and prefer to cache their experiences in shadowy silences, there seems little likelihood that the broader community will be encouraged to recognise and make redress for the gendered violence and abuse that was perpetrated by all sides during the years of conflict.

But at another level, this scenario also says something critical about the way the broader women, peace and security agenda has been re-articulated on Bougainville to frame women's accounts of peacebuilding. Efforts to defy gendered victimhood by shining light and heat on women's peacebuilding agency may be presently in vogue globally[64] and a source of comfort when we apply a gendered lens to conflict analysis. But if we develop this analysis in ways that also cast obscuring shadows over women's experiences of victimhood as peacebuilders, we over-romanticise this activity as an unreserved feminised good. As the testimonies I gathered in Bougainville suggest, instead of generating light and heat, this frictional encounter between the global and local, may be a dangerous overexposure that effaces the risks women may also be forced to navigate in peace-mediation work. It may also discourage female peace agents who have been exposed to violence from presenting themselves simultaneously as victims of abuse and entitled recipients of recognition and justice.

---

[62]Anonymous source, Interview with author, Buka, June 17, 2014.

[63]See earlier discussion of how ideas about the need to protect Bougainvillean women motivated men to become involved in initial resistance activity against the mine, p. 5.

[64]See e.g. Albrecht Schnabel and Anara Tabyshalieva, *Defying Victimhood: Women and Post-Conflict Peacebuilding* (Tokyo: United Nations University Press, 2012).

Conclusion

Women's contributions to peacebuilding in Bougainville are universally acknowledged by researchers, policy-makers and the local community. My own work on Bougainville indicated to me that women leaders in Bougainville were proud of their work in this capacity and eager to remind all who cared to listen about its validity. But this is a complex story, the nuances of which are not clearly illuminated at first glance. Local women leaders may have seized upon the UNSCR 1325 policy framework to further highlight their agency in conflict and to assist their struggles to be part of longer term conflict transition processes. But, as I have shown, this interleaving of global and local influences seems also to have encouraged a highly feminised and fetishised account of women's conflict experiences that shine frictional light and heat on some elements but cast other more complex realities into shadows.

On the one hand, the focus on women's peace leadership has ensured that women peacebuilders' successes, particularly as they pertain to the negotiation of 'bottom-up' peacebuilding, remain in the spotlight. On the other hand, this lens seems to discourage recognition of women's involvement in the resistance movement, women's critical political contributions at various stages of the conflict, and how this evidence of political acumen might be drawn upon to assist women's future contributions to the post-conflict political landscape.

This focus on women's peacebuilding agency also obscures the experiences of violence and intimidation that sometimes accompanied women peace leaders' work, making agents of peace also victims of violence. This is a disturbing counter-narrative in itself, but also concerning for the ways that the light and heat narrative of women's peacebuilding is constructed so that it appears to cast these darker experiences into shadowy obscurity.

The 'light and heat' friction that has given shape to contemporary accounts of women's leadership in Bougainville has captured the imagination of local and international peacebuilders and those in the region who work to promote awareness of the WPS framework. More attention focused on women's particular capacities to resolve disputes will, it is true, provide strong anchors for a sustainable peace in Bougainville. But more attention also needs to be paid the experiences which shadow this story. Without this, women's peacebuilding risks being invoked in fragmentary and fetishised forms. These may lack nuance, and offer only modest resources to assist women's broader advancement in the post-conflict context.

Disclosure statement

No potential conflict of interest was reported by the author.

Funding

This work was supported by the Australian Research Council Discovery Early Career Research Award [DE130100099].

'What is wrong with men?': revisiting violence against women in conflict and peacebuilding

Donna Pankhurst

Peace Studies, University of Bradford, Bradford, UK

ABSTRACT
Much has been written about the high rates of rape and other forms of violence against 'enemy' women in wartime and sustained violence against women in post-war contexts. Research on violence against women, recognised as a problem for peace and development and even a threat to international security, has begun to identify and explain contrasts between different locations. The explanations focus on men, their behaviour and 'masculinities', some of which, and even some military codes, may even proscribe such violence. By contrast, research on the mental health of male former combatants, and possibly other male survivors of war trauma, suggests that there is a strong risk of them perpetrating violence specifically against women, even in cases where the highest standard of veteran care is expected, but without much explanation. This article considers what potential there is in this topic for lessons in peacebuilding policy and identifies areas for future research.

Much has been written about the high rates of rape and other forms of sexual violence committed by men against 'enemy' women in wartime. There is a veritable canon of feminist academic work on the nature of, and explanations for, such violence in war.[1] Brownmiller[2] paved the way in the 1970s to seeing sexual violence in war as being committed by men *qua* men against women *qua* women, as war provides the opportunity, and that it is ubiquitous, whether or not it is condoned or used by political forces. A 'second wave' of feminist work has demonstrated the complexity of wartime sexual violence and its variation; has considered a wider range of explanations; and has articulated why this phenomenon is a security

---

[1] A useful list of 'the canon' up to the 1990s is set out in reference 7 of Inger Skjelsbæk, 'Sexual Violence and War: Mapping Out a Complex Relationship', *European Journal of International Relations* 7, no 2 (2001): 211–37. To this I would add: Sheila Meintjes, Anu Pillay and Meredeth Turshen, eds., The Aftermath: Women in *Post - Conflict Transformation* (London: Zed Press, Moser, 2001); Caroline Moser and Fiona C. Clark, eds., *Victims, Perpetrators or Actors? Gender, Armed Conflict and Political Violence* (London: Zed Books, 2001); Caroline Nordstrom, *Girls and Warzones. Troubling Questions* (Uppsala: Life and Peace Institute, 1997); and D. Buss, 'Rethinking "Rape as a weapon of War"', *Feminist Legal Studies* 17 (2009): 145–63. A thoughtful review of this evidence is at, Anette Bringedal Houge, 'Sexualised War Violence. Knowledge Construction and Knowledge Gaps', *Aggression and Violent Behaviour* 25 (2015): 79–87.

[2] Her seminal work is, Against Our Will: Men, Women and Rape (New York: Fawcett Books, 1975) which has been re-published many times and in different countries.

issue.[3] In the policy arena, there is nonetheless a persistent view of men's generalised predilection to commit acts of sexual violence against women, as promoted by Brownmiller. This is the case in the 'Women, Peace and Security' agenda of the UN (WPS),[4] and the policy approaches taken by many other international organisations which have aligned their work to it.[5] The WPS agenda calls for the mainstreaming of gender into activities relating to post-conflict peacebuilding, but does not easily take on the insights from the 'second-wave' of feminist work.

This article is therefore written in response to Richmond and MacGinty's suggestion that 'it would be useful to integrate gender analysis more fully into our research'.[6] In particular, here I attempt to show peacebuilding scholars the outcome of some aspects of the 'second wave' of feminist, and other, research on violence against women, which may be helpful for post-war peacebuilding. These include explanations for the continuation of sexual violence in peacebuilding settings,[7] and what is known about the behaviours of men who may be spoilers of peace, and how they are conceptualised and explained.

Violence against women as a problem for peacebuilding

The WPS agenda was established in response to feminist campaigning along three broad lines. First, there was an argument that women experience specific forms of violence, that tend to be overlooked, and therefore require special attention. Second, these campaigns posited that there is something specific (if not unique) about these violence in war and post-war settings, as compared with non-war settings (although the decades of research on the latter are rarely considered).[8] Third, there is a foundational assumption that women have something distinct from men to offer in peacebuilding, but are almost universally marginalised, and often absent, from peace talks and other peacebuilding activities, which leads to their rights and interests being marginalised or even undermined in peacebuilding.

The assumptions regarding the distinctiveness of such violence have been subject to critical comment by feminist writers[9] who critiqued the assumption that women would be more successful at peacebuilding as an essentialist view of women, and the view that they are more innately peaceful and have special skills and abilities to prevent violence if they are given the opportunity – seeing 'peace as women's work'.[10] The focus on women (as victims, survivors, activists and leaders) sometimes eclipsed the analysis of men. Furthermore, an

---

[3]For example, L. Anderson, 'Politics by Other Means: When does Sexual Violence Threaten International Peace and Security?', *International Peacekeeping* 17, no. 2 (2010): 244–60; and L. Sjoberg, 'Seeing Sex, Gender, and Sexuality in International Security', *International Journal* 70, no. 3 (2015): 1–20.

[4]The eight UN security council resolutions under the WPS framework may be found at http://www.un.org/en/peacekeeping/issues/women/wps.shtml (accessed February 3, 2016).

[5]See Susan Willett, 'Introduction: Security Council Resolution 1325: Assessing the Impact on Women, Peace and Security', *International Peacekeeping* 17, no. 2 (2010): 142–58, and the other articles in this issue.

[6]Oliver P. Richmond and Roger MacGinty, 'Where now for the Critique of the Liberal Peace?', *Cooperation and Conflict* 50, no. 2 (2015): 184.

[7]I use the terms *post-war* and *peacebuilding* throughout but with the usual caveats that such phases are rarely clear-cut temporally, or chronological. I use *war* rather than *conflict* as the latter covers many different contexts that are not related to war in any way, but also acknowledge that there are many different types and definitions of war.

[8]A very useful review is Beverly A. McPhail, 'Feminist Framework Plus: Knitting Feminist Theories of Rape Etiology into a Comprehensive Model', *Trauma Violence Abuse* 17, no. 3 (May 2015): 314–329, doi:10.1177/152483801558436; see also F. Miler, 'Rape: Sex Crime, Act of Violence, or Naturalistic Adaptation?', *Aggression and Violent Behavior* 19 (2014): 67–81.

[9]See note 1 above, and Azza Karam 'Women in War and Peace-building: The Roads Traversed, The Challenges Ahead', *International Feminist Journal of Politics* 3, no. 1 (2000): 2–25.

[10]See note 1 above.

over-focus on sexual violence has sometimes obscured the other violence experienced by women (and men), which may also be considered to be more serious by women survivors.[11]

Sexual violence covers a range of acts and is variously defined in different legal settings. The introduction to an important database on violence in conflict follows the definitions of the International Criminal Court:

> we define sexual violence as (1) rape, (2) sexual slavery, (3) forced prostitution, (4) forced pregnancy, and 5) forced sterilization/abortion. Following Elisabeth Wood (2009), we also include (6) sexual mutilation, and (7) sexual torture. This definition does not exclude the existence of female perpetrators and male victims, both of which are observed in the data. We focus on violations that involve direct force and/or physical violence. We exclude acts that do not go beyond verbal sexual harassment, abuse or threats, including sexualised insults, forced nudity, or verbal humiliation.[12]

This database clearly illustrates that there is considerable variety in the prevalence of sexual violence, as well as other factors, rather than being ubiquitous. It has facilitated the identification of correlations between different possible explanatory factors during war on a large quantitative scale,[13] including typologies of war,[14] although there is not yet a consensus on what the typologies should be. It includes data for five years after the official ending of conflict,[15] with much potential for the future analysis of peacebuilding.

A great deal more attention is paid to sexual violence against women than other violence against them, and even sometimes women or even men's deaths, both during and after conflict. Sexual violence can of course lead to death (immediately, through HIV or other injuries resulting in death[16]) but often it does not, hence the large numbers of women (and smaller numbers of men) who give testimony as survivors. A question for our time is why sexual violence is held up as the ultimate war damage – by some commentators almost worse than death.[17] At times, it seems almost salacious[18] when women themselves sometimes see other issues (including violence) as being more important. These include domestic violence, and

---

[11]Karam, 'Women in War and Peace-building', 2–25.

[12]Dara Kay Cohen and Ragnhild Nordås, *Sexual Violence in Armed Conflict (SVAC) Data-set Codebook and User Instruction Guide* (2013) www.sexualviolencedata.org. Further clarification of rape is also given (p. 7), 'Rape is defined as the case where the perpetrator invaded the body of a person by conduct resulting in penetration, however slight, of any part of the body of the victim or of the perpetrator with a sexual organ, or of the anal or genital opening of the victim with any object or any other part of the body. The invasion was committed by force, or by threat of force or coercion, such as that caused by fear of violence, duress, detention, psychological oppression or abuse of power, against such person or another person, or by taking advantage of a coercive environment, or the invasion was committed against a person incapable of giving genuine consent', along with definitions of other acts listed. Also see D.K. Cohen, 'Explaining Rape during Civil War: Cross-National Evidence (1980–2009)', *American Political Science Review* 107, no. 3 (2013): 461–77.

[13]Cohen and Nordås, *Sexual Violence in Armed Conflict.*

[14]DaraKayCohenandRagnhildNordås,SexualViolenceinArmedConflict(SVAC)Data-setCodebookandUserInstructionGuide(2013) http://www.sexualviolencedata.org

[15]Cohen and Nordås, *Sexual Violence in Armed Conflict*, 8. The data are drawn from the State Department, Amnesty International, and Human Rights Watch.

[16]Thomas Plumper and Eric Neumayer, 'The Unequal Burden of War: the Effect of Armed Conflict on the Gender Gap in Life Expectancy', *International Organization* 60, no. 3 (July 2006): 723–54.

[17]For example, 'Women and girls are uniquely and disproportionately affected by armed conflict. Women bear the brunt of war and are the vast majority of casualties resulting from war', http://www.amnestyusa.org/our-work/issues/women-s-rights/women-peace-and-security.

[18]"'It is really amazing", said one Kosovar woman … "that the international community cared only about Kosovar women when they were being raped – and then only as some sort of exciting story. We see now that they really don't give a damn about us." Elisabeth Rehn and Ellen Johnson Sirleaf, *Women, War and Peace: The Independent Experts' Assessment on the Impact of Armed Conflict on Women and Women's Role in Peace-building* (New York: UNIFEM, 2002), 125. This view was echoed by feminist activists, academics and policy makers at an international conference held by the Sexual Violence in Armed Conflict research group in Hamburg, July 2015.

public attacks on individual or groups of women, as well as features of structural violence such as land rights, property rights, employment and political representation.

Men as well as women are targeted for violence because of their gender. It is after all normal in wartime for forces to target young men and in some wars the focus is on all men, as they are seen as the most obvious threat and even to define the enemy. Death from immediate assault is always a more common outcome for men than for women[19] (even though some feminist activists persist in referring to women as the greater victims of war). There is some nuance to the relative death rates of men and women if longer-term causes of death caused by war are taken into account, but it is pretty much universally the case that, at the end of wars, women outnumber men.

Addressing sexual violence should be part of post-war peacebuilding for several reasons which go beyond the basic legal and moral issues. It may become a security issue.[20] It causes major ruptures in society (among men as well as between women, men and children) at a time when it is hoped that families can contribute to social stability.[21] Persistent impunity for perpetrators undermines government legitimacy, whereas impartial prosecution can reinforce it. At a practical level, it can reduce the potential for economic activity, particularly that of women and girls at a time when this is seen as crucial, particularly in rural economies reliant on their labour for agriculture.[22]

As a means of addressing these and other gender issues, the WPS agenda calls for the 'mainstreaming of gender' in all aspects of peacebuilding, and so international organisations have aligned their position accordingly. Both NGOs working at a local level,[23] and academic analyses,[24] have highlighted the significance for development and peace of reducing violence against women, as well as the promotion of equality between women and men. There is a large and growing body of work which highlights the failure to achieve the ambitions of WPS, which tend to conclude that local and international structures of power continue to prevent women playing the roles called for in the WPS, but that local analyses are needed to uncover what is going on given the considerable variations.[25]

The phenomenon of post-war violence against women after wars

In the peacebuilding phase, it is also common to see heightened rates of violence committed by men against 'their own' (i.e. non-enemy) women, whether they be spouses, other known

---

[19]E.G. Krug et al., eds., *World report on Violence and Health* (Geneva: World Health Organization, 2002).

[20]Anderson, 'Politics by Other Means'.

[21]R. Jenkins and A. Goetz, 'Addressing Sexual Violence in Internationally Mediated Peace Negotiations', *International Peacekeeping* 17, no. 2 (2010): 261–77, especially 266; and D. Buss et al., eds., *Sexual Violence in Conflict and Post-Conflict Societies: International Agendas and African Contexts* (London: Routledge, 2014).

[22]R. Jenkins and A. Goetz, 'Addressing Sexual Violence in Internationally Mediated Peace Negotiations', *InternationalPeace keeping* 17, no. 2 (2010): 261–77, especially 266; and D. Buss et al., eds., *Sexual Violence in Conflict and Post-ConflictSocieties: International Agendas and African Contexts* (London: Routledge, 2014).

[23]For example, ACORD, 2016 http://www.acordinternational.org/news/violence-against-women-and-girls--a-development-issue/.

[24]For example, Jenkins and Goertz, 'Addressing Sexual Violence'; and Buss et al., *Sexual Violence in Conflict*.

[25]For example, F. Ní Aoláin, D.F. Haynes, and N.R. Cahn, *On the Frontlines: Gender, War, and the Post-Conflict Process* (New York: Oxford University Press, 2011); T. Gizelis and L. Olsson, eds., *Gender, Peace and Security: Implementing UN Security Council Resolution 1325* (London: Routledge, 2015); M. McWilliams and A. Kilmurray, 'From the Global to the Local: Grounding UNSCR 1325 on Women, Peace and Security in Post Conflict Policy Making', *Women's Studies International Forum* 51 (2015): 128–35; and A. Björkdahl and J. Mannergren Selimovic, 'Translating UNSCR 1325 from the Global to the National: Protection, Representation and Participation in the National Action Plans of Bosnia-Herzegovina and Rwanda', *Conflict, Security and Development* 15 (2015): 311–35.

men, or strangers. Literature on the 'backlash' or 'aftermath' of war locates these bodily violence against women within a broader set of actions by men which work against women post-war. These actions can be supported by, or even led by, the state, and cover a range from disadvantageous legislation and policy to acceptance of everyday abuses (sexual and otherwise) in private and public which undermine women's status, as well as actual harm. Some may not even include sexual violence,[26] whilst other contexts, such as Guatemala, have witnessed such heightened rates of post-war violence against women, often resulting in death, that the term *femicide* is used.[27]

Perhaps because of the widespread publicity about high levels of sexual violence during the Rwandan genocide and the former-Yugoslavian wars, it is common to assume that sexual violence is particularly high in ethnic-based wars, and in the context of ethnic cleansing. When more case studies are analysed, however, this correlation is not born out and is certainly therefore not inevitable.[28] Sierra Leone's war, for example, is known to have had high rates of sexual violence but could not accurately be described as an ethnic conflict.

There is huge variation in the nature, extent and longevity of the backlash, and the patterns do not seem obviously to match women's experiences during war. Commentators locate 'backlash violence against women' within the context of a reaction to changed gender norms,[29] but the earlier tendency to generalise is countered by the emergent picture of enormous variety in women's experiences after war. This type of backlash violence can occur at a high level where there was not a major change in women's roles, and in some where gender relations did change significantly, this is not followed by mass increases of violence against women.[30]

An important example of an attempt to look in detail at this violence was published some time ago by Judy El-Bushra.[31] In Northern Uganda, women were provided with income-generating opportunities that were not open to men and it was reported to researchers by both that increases in violence against women have been triggered by men's resentment about the loss of their role as provider and their new-found dependence on women.[32] By contrast, El-Bushra reports that in Angola, men accepted their wives' economic dominance without this violent response. The explanation for such variety is not present in an analysis which only considers the change in gender relations and deduces this to be the cause in men's behaviour.

'Masculinity' as explanatory factor: 'What is wrong with men?'

Feminist writers have in the past located heightened levels of violence, and particularly sexual violence against women, within the conceptual framework of 'masculinity'. The

---

[26]For example, Elisabeth Jean Wood 'Variation in Sexual Violence during War', *Politics & Society* 34, no. 3 (September 2006): 307–42; and Elisabeth Jean Wood, 'Armed Groups and Sexual Violence: When Is Wartime Rape Rare?', *Politics and Society* 37, no. 1 (2009): 131–62.

[27]See H. Trujillo, 'Femicide and Sexual Violence in Guatemala', in *Terrorizing Women: Feminicide in the Américas*, eds. Rosa-Linda Fregoso and Cynthia Bejarano (Durham: Duke UP, 2010), 127–37.

[28]Also see D.K. Cohen, 'Explaining Rape during Civil War: Cross-National Evidence (1980–2009)'.

[29]For example, Meintjes, Pillay and Turshen, *The Aftermath*; and Meredeth Turshen and Alidou Ousseina, 2000. 'Africa: Women in the Aftermath of Civil War', *Race and Class* 41, no. 4 (2001): 81–92.

[30]Wood, 'Variation in Sexual Violence during War', 325.

[31]J. El-Bushra, 'Fused in Combat: Gender Relations and Armed Conflict', *Development in Practice* 13 (2003): 2–3, 252–65; see also C. Dolan, 'Collapsing Masculinities and Weak States – A Case Study of Northern Uganda', in *Masculinities Matter! Men, Gender and Development*, ed. Frances Cleaver (London: Zed Books, 2000), 57–83; and M. Turshen, 'The Political Economy of Rape: An Analysis of Systematic Rape and Sexual Abuse of Women during Armed Conflict in Africa'; and Moser and Clark, *Victims, Perpetrators Or Actors?*

[32]Jenkins and Goertz, 'Addressing Sexual Violence', 266 make the same point.

word alone is used in many different ways and so it is important to be clear about what is intended. At its simplest, it merely refers to what men do, within a socially approved framework. Various prefixes have sometimes been used to highlight the nature of a new specific set of behaviours and beliefs, such as *extreme-masculinity*, or *hyper-masculinity*.[33] The intellectual heritage of *hegemonic masculinity* is the careful scholarship undertaken by Connell and others[34] in which the concept has been developed.[35] Hegemonic masculinity refers not necessarily to the set of beliefs and practices that all men are expected to embody and perform, but what is aspired to; it is an expression of normativity. This is a complex and much-debated topic with interesting reflections about the extent to which hegemonic masculinity changes, and why and how, in different settings.

Crucially, there are attempts to tie together the practical and actually existing efforts of men and women, in their roles as political leaders, community leaders, wives and mothers, for example, to change what is expected of men – using exhortation, but also punishment for non-compliance. Typically, shame is used.[36] One of the complexities of this concept is that to be hegemonic, the normative values of masculinity have to be supported and sanctioned socially rather than enforced, when this is evidently not always the case, and would require widespread endorsement from women.

Integral to the concept of *hegemonic masculinity* is the notion that different *subordinate* masculinities coexist in the same setting, where the meaning is less ideological and more about being and doing. Not all men are expected to be the strongest, most violent, most successful, by definition, and so alternative masculinities exist which are more widely attainable. Without considerable care, the use of the term in this setting is little more than a descriptive label and does not give any further explanatory power than *gender roles* or *gendered identities*. It can also be tautologous: men behave like this because their masculinity makes them behave like this, and their masculinity is determined by their maleness and what men do. Such an approach can also lead to a crude essentialism about maleness which is not accurate or helpful in seeking to understand the nature and causes of variety and differentiation between different men's behaviours.

In particular, it is often suggested that men, passively or actively, fall under the pressures of changed masculinities which take on extreme forms.[37] More recent research tends not to rely heavily on the use of 'masculinities' as a concept[38] but focuses on the variability of incidence of sexual violence, and the importance of analysing the specificities of social context.

---

[33]See Donna Pankhurst, 'Post-War Backlash Violence against Women: What Can "Masculinity" Explain?', in *Gendered Peace: Women's Struggles for Post-War Justice and Reconciliation*, ed. D. Pankhurst (Oxon: Routledge, 2007), 293–320.

[34]R.W. Connell, *Masculinities* (Berkeley, CA: California Press, 2005); Michael S. Kimmel, Jeff Hearn and Robert W. Connell, eds., *Handbook of Studies on Men and Masculinities* (London: Sage, 2005); Jeff Hearn, *The Violences of Men* (London: Sage, 1998).

[35]R.W. Connell and James W. Messerschmidt, 'Hegemonic Masculinity: Rethinking the Concept', *Gender and Society* 19, no. 6 (2005): 829–59.

[36]It is very common for women to publicly seek to shame men who are reluctant to fight, such as the presenting of white feathers in public during the First World War in the UK, and see Jamie Munn, 'The Hegemonic Male and Kosovar Nationalism, 2000–2005', *Men and Masculinities* 10, no. 4 (June 2008): 440–56.

[37]For example, Euan Hague, 'Rape, Power and Masculinity: The Construction of Gender and National Identities in the War in Bosnia-Herzegovina', in *Gender and Catastrophe*, ed. Ronit Lentin (London: Zed Press, 1997), 50–63. Who uses *heteronational masculinity*; and see Pankhurst, 'Post-War Backlash Violence', for further comment on the usefulness of the term.

[38]For example, Cohen, 'Explaining Rape during Civil War'; Cohen and Nordås, *Sexual Violence in Armed Conflict*; and J. Gottschall, 'Explaining Wartime Rape', *The Journal of Sex Research* 41, no. 2 (2004): 129–36.

Research with men in Sierra Leone[39] and DRC[40] has revealed greater understanding of local experiences and suggests that the reasons are varied, even within the same contexts.[41] In some settings, for instance, there is a stronger tendency for official, state-supported forces to commit sexual violence than militias or rebel groups, rather than all men.[42] In some, women are also perpetrators of a range of violence[43] whilst in others to a far lesser degree or not at all.

Connecting the study of masculinities to the study of sexual violence

In some cases, men also experience specifically sexual violence, although there are key differences in the way this is categorised.[44] Men suffer much violence which is referred to as torture but which focuses on the genitalia and/or is aimed at preventing future procreation, and so therefore could well be described as sexual violence (and of course the sexual violence that women experience may also be categorised as torture). Whilst it is commonly believed that men's reporting is probably even lower than that of women, it is not generally thought to feature as a post-war phenomenon,[45] even though one can speculate on its impact on men's mental health in the longer term.

---

[39]Interestingly Cohen 'Explaining Rape during Civil War' shows that committing rape in the Sierra Leone war was known to be very dangerous for the perpetrator, where debilitating STDs are common, including HIV/Aids.

[40]Maria Eriksson Baaz and Maria Stern, 'Why do Soldiers Rape? Masculinity, Violence and Sexuality in the Armed Forces in the Congo (DRC)', *International Studies Quarterly* 53, no. 2 (2009): 495–518; and Theo Hollander, 'Men, Masculinities, and the Demise of a State: Examining Masculinities in the Context of Economic, Political, and Social Crisis in a Small Town in the Democratic Republic of the Congo', *Men and Masculinities* 17, no. 4 (2014): 417–39. In addition, the high levels of sexual violence in DRC has attracted more detailed studies from various disciplines than most other recent, see for instance: S.A. Bartels et al., 'Sexual Violence Trends between 2004 and 2008 in South Kivu, Democratic Republic of Congo', *Prehospital and Disaster Medicine* 26 (2011): 408; S. Bartels et al., 'Militarized Sexual Violence in South Kivu, Democratic Republic of Congo', *Journal of Interpersonal Violence* 28 (2013): 340–58; Françoise Duroch, Melissa McRae, and Rebecca F. Grais. 'Description and Consequences of Sexual Violence in Ituri Province, Democratic Republic of Congo', *BMC International Health and Human Rights* 11, no. 1 (2011); M. Guimond and K. Robinette, 'A Survivor behind Every Number: Using Programme Data on Violence against Women and Girls in the Democratic Republic of Congo to Influence Policy and Practice', *Gender and Development* 22 (2014): 311–26; T. Hecker et al., 'Appetitive Aggression in Former Combatants – Derived from the Ongoing Conflict in DR Congo', *International Journal of Law and Psychiatry* 35 (2012): 244–9; J. Kelly et al., '"If Your Husband Doesn't Humiliate You, Other People Won't": Gendered Attitudes towards Sexual Violence in Eastern Democratic Republic of Congo', *Global Public Health* 7 (2012): 285–98; R. Kidman, T. Palermo, and J. Bertrand, 'Intimate Partner Violence, Modern Contraceptive Use and Conflict in the Democratic Republic of the Congo', *Social Science and Medicine* 133 (2015): 2–10; B. Maclin et al., '"They Have Embraced a Different Behaviour": Transactional Sex and Family Dynamics in Eastern Congo's Conflict", *Culture, Health and Sexuality* 17 (2015): 119–31; S. Meger 'Rape of the Congo: Understanding Sexual Violence in the Conflict in the Democratic Republic of Congo', *Journal of Contemporary African Studies* 28 (2010): 119–35; J. Trenholm et al., 'Constructing Soldiers from Boys in Eastern Democratic Republic of Congo', *Men and Masculinities* 16 (2013): 203–27; and G. Zihindula and P. Maharaj, 'Risk of Sexual Violence: Perspectives and Experiences of Women in a Hospital in the Democratic Republic of Congo', *Journal of Community Health* 40 (2015): 736–43. This was also historically the case amongst US forces in Vietnam. For example, in the My Lai massacre, not all men engaged in the sexual violence and killing of women and children, according to their own testimonies to US Congress (https://www.loc.gov/rr/frd/Military_Law/Vol_II-testimony.html).

[41]Baaz and Stern, 'Why do Soldiers Rape?'; and Maria Eriksson Baaz and Maria Stern, *Sexual Violence as a Weapon of War? Perceptions, Prescriptions, Problems in the Congo and Beyond* (London: Zed Books, 2013), 5.

[42]Dara Kay Cohen and Ragnhild Nordås, 'Sexual Violence in Armed Conflict: Introducing the SVAC Data-set, 1989–2009', *Journal of Peace Research* 5, no. 3 (2014): 418–28; Jennifer L. Green, 'Uncovering Collective Rape: A Comparative Study of Political Sexual Violence', *International Journal of Sociology* 34, no. 1 (2004): 97–116.

[43]Susie Jacobs, Ruth Jacobson and Jennifer Marchbank, eds., *States of Conflict. Gender, Violence and Resistance* (London: Zed Books, 2000); and see also Sjoberg and Gentry's *Mothers, Monsters, Whores* (London: Zed Books, 2007).

[44]Sandesh Sivakumaran, 'Sexual Violence Against Men in Armed Conflict', *European Journal of International Law* 18, no. 2 (2007): 253–76.

[45]For an account of how this is embedded within combat, see P. Kirby, 'Ending Sexual Violence in Conflict: the Preventing Sexual Violence Initiative and its Critics', *International Affairs* 91 (2015): 3.

Yet in spite of the variety, where sexual violence does occur, it is also seen as being at the heart of gender identity for women and men, even when they include acts which happen to both, such as the stripping of clothes, and anal and oral rape. At the same time, these acts during conflict are thought to constitute attacks on more than the individual and to hold a power that goes beyond the immediate wounding and death, but are intended and experienced as attacks on the whole community in order to undermine morale and social order. This remains a much under-researched area in post-war settings.

There is still much to understand about the motivation of male perpetrators of sexual violence in the peacebuilding phase, just as there is during war. The loss of social values and psychological damage is generally presumed to be part of the explanation, summed up in the idea of a 'culture of violence', and it is also commonly described as a means of control or punishment, rather than sexual desire, but there is still far more scope for research with veterans/ex-combatants,[46] and what is considered best practice for recovery, as well as the impact of violent trauma on non-combatant men.

Writers vary in the degree to which they consider rape and sexual violence to be about sex, and very few writers draw on the research findings on these phenomena in non-war settings. The key historical feminist contribution to discussion of rape was to see that this is not about sex but an act of violence intended to control, demean or punish women within a system of patriarchy.[47] Alongside this view is the assumption that war heightens men's sex drive and also removes social constraints.[48] Clearly, the situation is often more complicated than this suggests, however, because of the significant variations in rates of incidence.[49]

A more nuanced approach considers the process of male sexual arousal and desire; penile rape cannot occur without an erection and it is alleged that many rapes end in ejaculation.[50] On the face of it, this reinforces the view that sexual violence is essentially about male desire, but the differences in men's behaviour at least brings this into question.[51] Sexual frustration and desire are less often cited as part of the explanation for sexual violence during peacebuilding than during war, but I am not aware of a study that specifically focuses on this 'wartime versus post-war' distinction. There is very little commentary, let alone research, on the ways in which shortened life expectancy and fear of death themselves may impact on sexual desire, or sexual activity in war, or peacebuilding.

Other attempts at explanations have considered the status of women and rates of sexual violence prior to war, but this also does not correlate neatly with high rates of sexual violence during war. In a few places, there was a deliberate attempt by leaders to prevent sexual crimes during war, which cuts across this explanation, such as in El Salvador.[52] The patterns then are complicated and certainly more so than individual opportunity or incentive, nor

---

[46]The terms former soldiers, ex-combatants, veterans and ex-fighters are used throughout the literature referring to locations other than the West. All but 'ex-fighters' are commonly used in the West.

[47]For a review of this literature, see Charlotte Watts and Cathy Zimmerman, 'Violence against Women: Global Scope and Magnitude', *The Lancet* 358 (April 6, 2002): 1232–7.

[48]Which I have previously cast as the 'social constraints removed thesis', Pankhurst 'Introduction', in *Gendered Peace: Women's Struggles for Post-War Justice and Reconciliation*, ed. D. Pankhurst (Oxon: Routledge, 2007), 1–30.

[49]Wood, 'Armed Groups and Sexual Violence', 135.

[50]Xabier Agirre Aranburu, 'Sexual Violence beyond Reasonable Doubt: Using Pattern Evidence and Analysis for International Cases', *Leiden Journal of International Law* 23 (2010): 614.

[51]Wood, 'Variation in Sexual Violence during War': 323–5.

[52]Wood, 'Armed Groups and Sexual Violence'.

can they be explained entirely by the strategic intentions of political or military leaders,[53] but require a nuanced and context-specific approach.

A more nuanced use of *masculinities* (however defined), occurs where they are used to describe, and even seek to explain, the ways in which some violence are effectively limited or even proscribed. Wood[54] highlights some commonly cited examples of wars where sexual violence is thought to have been limited precisely because of a masculinity promoted by military leaders that choose not to engage in such behaviour. If this is accomplished merely by a strict military code, however, it is not clear what the introduction of the *masculinities* concept adds to our understanding. Where it might do is where men have more choice and refuse – such as at an individual level when they choose not to conform to a norm with a high level of sexual violence.[55] In so doing, they are presumably embracing a different *masculinity* which tends to be ignored in such analyses, in the shadow of violence.

Wood[56] has developed a framework for describing the prevalence of sexual violence in war, having clearly illustrated that there is enormous variety. She and other writers[57] have also highlighted that the incidence of sexual violence can vary within wars, geographically and temporally, and so there is a great deal that needs explaining. Data on sexual violence are of course very difficult to verify (as it is in non-war settings), but she makes a strong case that the potential for under-reported incidence is very unlikely itself to explain the variation.[58] She emphasises this differentiation by highlighting some wars where sexual violence is thought to be very rare, for example, in El Salvador and Palestine/Israel, and where there is an asymmetrical prevalence of sexual violence between opposing sides, for example in Sri Lanka. She also sets out different levels at which such violence should be analysed; as part of a leadership or military strategy, at the group level, where it serves to build bonds between members; and finally at the individual level.

Wood's analysis is based on correlations, rather than explanations, which leaves in place the common assumption that if the right conditions are in place, then all men will undertake these acts.[59] This is not the case though, as it seems that it is never the case that all men do this. The differences between men's behaviour in the same contexts has received the least attention and yet is possibly the most potentially significant in our understanding of violence in peacebuilding phases.

Perhaps the most obvious parallel with the fighting group of men level of analysis in war, is post-war gangs, where sexual violence can also be part of initiation rites and continued status, and which are very common in post-war urban centres.[60] The same explanatory challenges apply at these levels, however, in that not all men behave in the same way and we do not have a clear understanding of what factors influence the variety of incidence. Opportunity and motivation are commonly suggested, including the use or threat of sexual violence in order to gain access to property; this is often described as 'sexual looting',

---

[53]Wood, 'Variation in Sexual Violence during War'; and Wood, 'Armed Groups and Sexual Violence', has made this case thoroughly through reviewing the SVLA data set.

[54]Wood, 'Armed Groups and Sexual Violence', 131–62.

[55]C. Enloe, 'When Soldiers Rape', in *Maneuvers: The International Politics of Militarizing Women's Lives*, ed. C. Enloe (London: University of California Press, 2000), 108–52.

[56]See note 54 above.

[57]For example, Inger Skjelsbæk, 'Sexual Violence and War'; and Dara Kay Cohen, 'Explaining Rape During Civil War: Cross-National Evidence (1980–2009)'.

[58]Wood, 'Armed Groups and Sexual Violence', 134.

[59]Wood, 'Variation in Sexual Violence during War': 321–7 outlines key features of opportunity and incentive.

[60]Cathy McIlwaine and Caroline O.N. Moser, 'Violence and Social Capital in Urban Poor Communities: Perspectives from Colombia and Guatemala', *Journal of International Development* 13, no. 7 (October 2001): 965–84.

particularly where women's property rights are insecure.[61] Davies and True usefully frame these issues within the need to keep at the forefront the analysis of gender relations in specific settings as it is these that determine the opportunities and incentives for men.[62] It is becoming clearer that there are key aspects of the context which seem to affect the chances and nature of such violence occurring and only with local knowledge can these be understood.[63]

One theme which occurs time and again is the mental health of men, whether they are former combatants or citizen survivors of violence (and people can be both at different moments during wars), and the suggestion that mental illness resulting from war may have something to do with acts of violence against women. Context is still very important here but there is a lot of potential to consider cross-cultural phenomena which may have some explanatory value as well as implications for policy.

What do we know of the impacts of war on male ex-combatants[64]

In the context of such variety of sexual violence, there is nonetheless a common focus on men who have been part of a military structure and/or committed and experienced high levels of violence.[65] Dating back to previous world wars, there is a broad expectation that levels of trauma are likely to lead to high levels of violence against women and many programmes for Disarmament, Demobilisation and Rehabilitation (DDR) acknowledge this, even if there is little attempt to address it.

Diagnosis is sometimes difficult, treatment is expensive and widely seen as unreliable,[66] and the specific connection with violence against women is not well understood. As a way of spotlighting what is known about this, it is worth considering the situation of war veterans from the UK and US armies. Both armies are highly influential in setting the expectations for international efforts to support former soldiers in countries emerging from war (as well as UN peacekeepers). In both the UK and USA, returning soldiers, and those who leave the service, experience disproportionately high levels of alcohol and drug use and engage in increased levels of domestic and social violence[67]. In the USA and the UK, there is not an explicit concern with the perpetration of violence against women per se, and data are not easily available to review the rates of these violence committed by veterans compared to the general population. Nonetheless, the mental health of combatants after active service is of serious concern to both armies, even though they have not been involved in civil wars, or face the problems of living in a post-war country, like many of the veterans who seem to present such a threat to peace elsewhere.

The US Army became so concerned that it made it mandatory for soldiers to report to officers if they suspect that a colleague is suffering from mental ill health.[68] There have been

---

[61]Aranburu, 'Sexual Violence Beyond Reasonable Doubt', 614; Turshen, 'The Political Economy of Rape: An Analysis of Systematic Rape and Sexual Abuse of Women During Armed Conflict in Africa'; and Moser and Clark, *Victims, Perpetrators Or Actors?*

[62]S. Davies and J. True, 'Reframing Conflict-related Sexual and Gender-based Violence: Bringing Gender Analysis Back in', *Security Dialogue* 46, no. 6 (2015): 495–512.

[63]Buss, 'Rethinking "Rape as a weapon of War"'.

[64]This is my focus for an ongoing research project.

[65]Pankhurst, 'Post-War Backlash Violence'.

[66]For example, David Wilson and Peter Barglow, 'PTSD Has Unreliable Diagnostic Criteria', *Psychiatric Times* 26, no. 7 (9 July, 2009): 30.

[67]For example, Patrick S. Calhoun et al., 'Hazardous Alcohol Use and Receipt of Risk-Reduction Counseling Among U.S. Veterans of the Wars in Iraq and Afghanistan', *Journal of Clinical Psychiatry* 69, no. 11 (2008): 1686–93; Amy D. Marshall, Jillian Panuzio, and Casey T. Taft, 'Intimate Partner Violence among Military Veterans and Active Duty Servicemen' *Clinical Psychology Review* 25, no. 7 (November 2005): 862–76.

[68]http://www.army.mil/article/154854; there many other articles available at http://www.army.mil/.

a number of major incidents where veterans have turned their weapons on their families on return from active duty, and data suggest that there is a higher level of domestic violence than in the general population.[69] There are also many accounts (much under-researched) from Vietnam veterans about the impact active service had on their mental health and what led them to commit violent crimes.[70]

There are sufficiently high numbers of UK soldiers in domestic prisons to have triggered a number of Freedom of Information requests by MPs and several official investigations.[71] There have been several inquiries about the high numbers of ex-soldiers in UK prisons – many of whom were committed for various crimes of assault, including domestic abuse.[72] One key report states that the majority of veteran prisoners have been committed for crimes of personal violence and that the majority of these are against women,[73] but the research concludes that there is no self-evident explanation for this. There has been a notable reluctance on the part of government to acknowledge the potential effects of war on soldiers[74] although there is official acknowledgement of the dangers of trauma for soldiers by the British Army,[75] and there has been little further investigation of this particular crime.

The medical research on PTSD has advanced but it is still seen as a complicated phenomenon with no clear medical consensus on treatment and certainly no broadly accepted position by western governments.[76] Proclamations about new attempts to take PTSD more seriously have also come into question, as ministers came to reject their own policy about psychological screening for mental illness[77] and soldiers report the stigma of acknowledging a problem whilst still in the army, which can lead to delays in visiting families and/or including the likelihood that they would have to leave the army, possibly with a dishonourable discharge, where violent crimes have been committed. Meanwhile, there are also concerns about the number of former soldiers who are homeless and/or unemployed.[78] Recent research on a small case sample in the UK focussing on domestic abuse against army wives by UK soldiers suggests that there is no correlation with perpetrators actual combat experience and that a lot of explanatory weight should be given to both the background of individuals and the experience of militarisation.[79]

---

[69]See note 65 above.

[70]Vietnam vets interviews cited in Wood, 'Variation in Sexual Violence during War'.

[71]C. Lyne and D. Packham, *The Needs of Ex-service Personnel in the Criminal Justice System: A Rapid Evidence Assessment* (London: Ministry of Justice Analytical Series, 2014); Howard League for Penal Reform, *Report of the Inquiry into Former Armed Service Personnel in Prison* (London: Howard League for Penal Reform, 2011); and Howard League for Penal Reform, *Leave No Veteran Behind. Inquiry into Former Armed Service personnel in Prison visits the United States of America* (London: Howard League for Penal Reform, 2011). Also see popular news coverage, http://www.dailymail.co.uk/news/article-1216015/More-British-soldiers-prison-serving-Afghanistan-shock-study-finds.html; http://www.guardian.co.uk/uk/2009/sep/24/jailed-veteran-servicemen-outnumber-troops.

[72]https://www.gov.uk/government/uploads/system/uploads/attachment_data/file/389855/the-needs-of-ex-service-personnel-in-the-cjs-rapid-evidence-assessment.pdf.

[73]Howard League, *Report of the Inquiry into Former Armed Service Personnel in Prison*.

[74]http://www.bbc.co.uk/programmes/b00sp1rv

[75]http://www.army.mod.uk/welfare-support/23245.aspx.

[76]Wilson and Barglow, 'PTSD Has Unreliable Diagnostic Criteria'; Kenneth E. Miller and Andrew Rasmussen, 'War Exposure, Daily Stressors, and Mental Health in Conflict and Post-Conflict Settings: Bridging the Divide Between Trauma-Focused and Psychosocial Frameworks', *Social Science and Medicine* 70 (2010): 7–16 show how the harm caused during conflict can continue beyond and propose new approaches to diagnosis and treatment.

[77]http://news.bbc.co.uk/1/hi/health/8739662.stm.

[78]http://www.mirror.co.uk/news/uk-news/9000-ex-service-personnel-homeless-after-2071049; http://news.stv.tv/west-central/190903-soldiers-on-the-streets-campaigners-sleep-rough-to-highlight-homelessness/; http://www.soldiersoffthestreet.com/How%20you%20can%20Help.html.

[79]H. Gray, 'Militarism in the Everyday: Responses to Domestic Abuse in the British Armed Forces' (PhD thesis, LSE, 2015).

Two key points could be taken from this very brief account of the US and UK. First, the decommissioned soldier/combatant, even in the best-resourced country of the world, can end up without any support for mental illness, and that this is likely to result in crimes of violence, as well as personal suffering including high rates of suicide for veterans themselves.[80] This is much more likely is this in poorer countries, whether men concerned were fighting for a government or an irregular army. As evidence accumulates, this phenomenon ought to figure more prominently in planning for peacebuilding.[81] Such a concern complements the feminist critiques of DDR which highlight the neglect of women's concerns.[82]

Once again, however, it is noteworthy that the impacts on fighting men are not universal or even consistent, and so there is still much to be learned about the men who commit these acts at an individual level, and those who do not. My initial review some years ago[83] showed that common psycho-social explanations tend to be ignored even in macrolevel analyses, and they have not fed into more detailed analyses of different local social, particularly gendered, post-war dynamics of violence. So the use of masculinities here was not very developed and did not assist in explanations of the variety. Specific local analyses are needed of gender roles and perhaps local, subordinate, masculinities and how they change. In many parts of the world, even if there was greater understanding of who is more likely to commit such violence, it would not increase the chances of preventive or therapeutic interventions as this is so expensive and is not often seen as a high priority compared with other violence-reduction measures.

Where such therapeutic interventions are attempted, they tend to be built on the Western model of individual, long-term psychiatric/therapy interventions, whilst there is a growing school of thought that this is not always the most appropriate approach and can sometimes exacerbate individual illness.[84] An alternative approach is thought to be more appropriate in some settings where people are counselled in group settings with the aim of rebuilding constructive relationships.[85] This is not just a 'cultural' difference between the West and the rest of the world as similar arguments have been put forward for emergency-personnel who survive traumatic events in the West.[86]

---

[80]http://www.telegraph.co.uk/news/uknews/defence/10178403/More-British-soldiers-commit-suicide-than-die-in-battle-figures-suggest.html.

[81]There is now a substantive body of research on the behaviour of male peacekeepers who engage in various forms of sexual violence against women, as well as prostitution, and abuse of children, e.g. P. Higate and M. Henry, 'Engendering (In)security in Peace Support Operations', *Security Dialogue* 35, no. 4 (December 2004): 481–98. They also draw the same conclusion that there is a tendency to overgeneralise about men's behaviour and that local context and knowledge is essential to understand the behaviour of peacekeepers.

[82]K.M. Jennings, 'The Political Economy of DDR in Liberia: A Gendered Critique', *Conflict, Security and Development* 9 (2009): 475–94; J.P. Kaufman and K.P. Williams, 'Women, DDR and Post-Conflict Transformation: Lessons from the Cases of Bosnia and South Africa', *Journal of Research in Gender Studies* 5 (2015): 11; Ní Aoláin et al., *On the Frontlines*; K. Theidon 'Reconstructing Masculinities: The Disarmament, Demobilization, and Reintegration of Former Combatants in Colombia', *Human Rights Quarterly* 31 (2009): 1–34; and W. Verkoren et al., 'From DDR To Security Promotion: Connecting National Programs To Community Initiatives', *International Journal of Peace Studies* 15 (2010): 1–32.

[83]See note 65 above.

[84]See Wilson and Barglow, 'PTSD Has Unreliable Diagnostic Criteria'.

[85]See Pankhurst, 'Post-War Backlash Violence'; and Anthony J. Marsella, 'Ethnocultural Aspects of PTSD: An Overview of Concepts, Issues, and Treatments', *Traumatology* 16, no. 4 (2010): 17–26.

[86]For example, Jerome Groopman, 'The Grief Industry How much does crisis counselling help—or hurt?', *New Yorker*, 2004, http://jeromegroopman.com/ny-articles/GriefIndustry-012604.pdf.

Conclusion

In parallel to the critics of 'Liberal Peace' provoking 'secondary critiques',[87] critics of the gendered nature of peace and peacebuilding have moved on from an earlier position of over-generalising about the extent and patterns of sexual violence, and the different roles played by women and men, to a newer acceptance of variability and the importance of context-specific explanation. Nonetheless, the amount of research undertaken is far greater on the incidence of violence against women during war than afterwards, or on the specifics of perpetration in context, or on its implications for peacebuilding. Whilst similar explanations are offered for sexual violence in both war and post-war contexts, there are additional phenomena at play in post-war settings, not least because violence against women is often committed by men from their own communities.

In this article, I have attempted to bring to the attention of those working on peacebuilding some of the key lessons of research about men's violence in post-war settings. Young men in particular are often seen as the most likely spoilers of peace, and men as a group are often held responsible for the key problems of inter-personal violence in peacebuilding settings, yet there is enormous variety in the ways that they behave. We know much more about violence in wartime than in post-war, although this is a fast-moving agenda, and we now have information about some of the variety and complexity of such phenomena. This ought to provoke us into taking more care not to make assumptions about 'self-evident' causes, or 'what is wrong with men', or to over-generalise about violence in post-war settings and how to minimise them.

There is now a range of explanations for different patterns of war and post-war violence which indicate complexity and context specificity, in much the same way that local contexts of broader aspects of peacebuilding require context-specific analyses. In this way, the discussion of post-war violence against women, and the possible approaches to deal with it as a peacebuilding issue, can be seen through the prism of the debate about the importance of 'the local' in the 'liberal peace' debates.

Several conclusions have significance for analysis and policy regarding post-war violence against women from this review. First, whilst wartime experiences are obviously significant in peacebuilding phases, there is no simple connection, just as the incidence of violence against women during wars is now recognised as being highly varied. A key lesson from analysis of wartime violence is that context is therefore very important and most generalised explanations do not hold in all contexts. That seems a simple thing to say but is important when considering the possible relevance of 'blueprint' approaches to peacebuilding.

Second, it is important to hold a spotlight to the men who do not commit such acts, as well as those who do, in order to better understand how the different drivers of opportunity and motivation play out. Within this context, the economic circumstances and other aspects of structural violence for men, as well as women, seem to be highly significant and so reconstruction strategies need to consider the impacts of promoting new economic opportunities for women at a fast rate, in the absence, or reduction, of those for men.

Lessons that may be learnt from the ways in which veteran fighters are treated in the UK and USA suggest that doing nothing to address mental health issues is likely to lead to high rates of violence against civilian women, whether or not mental ill health is caused by active combat. Furthermore, similar issues may occur amongst people who have not been

---

[87]Richmond and MacGinty, 'Where now for the Critique of the Liberal Peace?, 174.

part of military structures but who have experienced trauma from violent wartime experiences. This may also seem an evident truth, yet it is one which is not effectively addressed in policy terms anywhere.

Such analyses of violence should also support us in the tasks ahead to notice and analyse where men's behaviours and ambitions change away from violent strategies and towards a stronger engagement with peace endeavours that also support women's multiple forms of agency exhibited in conflict and post-conflict settings.

Disclosure statement

No potential conflict of interest was reported by the author.

Decolonising gender and peacebuilding: feminist frontiers and border thinking in Africa

Heidi Hudson

Centre for Africa Studies, University of the Free State, Bloemfontein, South Africa

ABSTRACT

The article seeks to theorise an integrated decolonised feminist frame for peacebuilding in an African context. Arguing that a decolonial-feminist lens has the potential to change the way we look at peacebuilding practices, I propose the notion of 'feminist frontiers' – an engaged yet stabilising heuristic tool for analysing racialised and gendered relations post-conflict. The argument is structured around three pillars, namely: *metageographies* as metaphoric mental-space constructions of a colonial peace; *masks* that constrain the introduction of complicated and intersected human subjecthoods; and *mundane matter* that elicits ambivalent engagements between human and post-human subjectivities in the areas of everyday political economies and infrastructural rule of peacebuilding. I conclude that such feminist frontiers represent intermediate and mediated spaces or epistemological borderlands from where the undertheorised and empirically understudied discursive and material dimensions of peacebuilding from a gender perspective can be investigated.

Over the last 20 years, a women and peacebuilding agenda has developed parallel to the evolution of a women, peace and security (WPS) agenda, with the two focus areas becoming largely entwined.[1] Currently, the debate has broadened to include a gender and peacebuilding emphasis.[2] However, I remain sceptical about the extent to which gender mainstreaming in peacebuilding has matured, especially because the conceptual and empirical conflation of women and gender persists. In the context of a thriving gender mainstreaming and peacebuilding industry, I have found that gender and peacebuilding funding proposals with an African focus frequently lack a normative commitment to gender sensitivity, fail

---

[1] Meredith Turshen and Clotilde Twagiramariya, eds., *What Women Do in Wartime: Gender and Conflict in Africa* (New York: Zed Books, 1998); Sheila Meintjes, Anu Pillay and Meredith Turshen, eds., *The Aftermath. Women in Post - Conflict Transformation* (London: Zed Books, 2001); Sanam Anderlini, *Women Building Peace. What They Do, Why It Matters* (London: Lynne Rienner, 2007); Elisabeth Porter, *Peacebuilding: Women in International Perspective* (London: Routledge, 2007); Donna Pankhurst, ed., *Gendered Peace. Women's Struggles for Post - War Justice and Reconciliation* (New York: Routledge, 2008); and Funmi Olonisakin, Karen Barnes and Eka Ikpe, *Women, Peace and Security. Translating Policy into Practice* (London: Routledge, 2011).

[2] Caroline Moser and Fiona Clark, eds., *Victims, Perpetrators or Actors? Gender, Armed Conflict and Political Violence* (London: Zed Books, 2001); Fionnuala D. Aoláin, Dina F. Haynes and Naomi Cahn, *On The Frontlines: Gender, War and the Post - Conflict Process* (Oxford: Oxford University Press, 2011); and Laura J. Shepherd, *Gender, Violence & Security. Discourse as Practice* (London: Zed Books, 2008).

BUILDING PEACE

to reflect an understanding of the complex power relations involved and are not guided by a feminist ethic or methodology. In such cases, mere opportunism to obtain a slice of the donor funding trumps all else. At the institutional level, despite having 'Women's Empowerment and Development towards Africa's Agenda 2063' as theme, high politics and security dominated the agenda of the African Union (AU) Summit in January 2015, crowding out not only an autonomous WPS agenda, but also any meaningful consideration of gender and security in general.

Although the flaws of liberal and post-liberal peacebuilding[3] and the flaws of the liberal-feminist inspired gender–peacebuilding nexus[4] are co-constituted, the aim of this article is not to revisit the feminist contention that a gender perspective can help liberate peacebuilding from its neoliberal shackles or that the exclusion of women from peacebuilding processes puts the whole project in jeopardy. Rather, the objective is to show how a multi-pronged 'feminist frontier' concept can invigorate gender and peacebuilding theorising in a way that does not entrench Eurocentric assumptions. Postcolonial-feminist writing on peacebuilding is fairly well developed,[5] but the exploration of gender and decoloniality in relation to peacebuilding remains underrepresented and undertheorised, with the literature focused on gender and coloniality generally.[6] Moreover, theories of decoloniality offer scathing critiques of modernity and its liberal projects, but lack an integral gender perspective.[7] For instance, although Meera Sabaratnam provides instructive suggestions on how to dismantle the liberal peace without using the master's tools, her contribution does not employ a gender lens.[8] With this in mind, the article seeks to make a theoretical contribution by challenging the conceptual delinking of gender and feminism in peacebuilding, the conflation of gender and sex and the centrality of (Eurocentric) liberalism to the whole mix.

Taking my cue from this work, I therefore explore feminist strategies to disrupt the conventional gender and peacebuilding consensus. And since my focus will be peacebuilding in an African context, the conceptualisation of decoloniality through the lens of feminist frontiers will commence with and draw on the mutually constitutive nature of racialised and gendered relations in the postcolony. I view peacebuilding as a network of gendered

---

[3] Mark R. Duffield, *Global Governance and the New Wars: The Merging of Development and Security* (New York: Zed Books, 2001); David Chandler, 'The Uncritical Critique of "Liberal Peace"', *Review of International Studies* 36 (2010): 137–55; and Oliver P. Richmond, 'The Problem of Peace: Understanding the "liberal peace"' *Conflict, Security & Development* 6, no. 3 (2006): 291–314.

[4] Shepherd, *Gender, Violence & Security*; Nicola Pratt and Sophie Richter-Devroe, 'Critically Examining UNSCR 1325 on Women, Peace and Security', *International Feminist Journal of Politics* 13, no. 4 (2011): 489–503; Heidi Hudson, 'A Double-edged Sword of Peace? Reflections on the Tension between Representation and Protection in Gendering Liberal Peacebuilding', *International Peacekeeping* 19, no. 4 (2012): 443–60; and Lesley Pruitt, '"Fixing the Girls": Neoliberal Discourse and Girls' Participation in Peacebuilding', *International Feminist Journal of Politics* 15, no. 1 (2013): 58–76.

[5] Amanda Chisholm, 'The Silenced and Indispensible. Gurkhas in Private Military Security Companies', *International Feminist Journal of Politics* 16, no. 1 (2014): 26–47; Julia Welland, 'Liberal Warriors and the Violent Colonial Logics of "Partnering and Advising"', *International Feminist Journal of Politics* 17, no. 2 (2015): 289–307.

[6] María Lugones, 'The Coloniality of Gender', *Worlds & Knowledges Otherwise* 2, Dossier 2, Spring (2008): 1–17; María Lugones, 'Toward a Decolonial Feminism', *Hypatia* 25, no. 4 (2010): 742–59; and Freya Schiwy, 'Decolonization and the Question of Subjectivity', *Cultural Studies* 21, no. 2–3 (2007): 271–94.

[7] Walter D. Mignolo, 'Coloniality of Power and De-colonial Thinking', *Cultural Studies* 21, no. 2–3 (2007): 155–67; Arturo Escobar, 'Beyond the Third World: Imperial Globality, Global Coloniality and Anti-Globalisation Social Movements', *Third World Quarterly* 25, no. 1 (2004): 207–30; and Sabelo Ndlovu-Gatsheni, *Empire, Global Coloniality and African Subjectivity* (New York: Berghahn, 2013).

[8] Meera Sabaratnam, 'IR in Dialogue … But Can We Change the Subjects? A Typology of Decolonizing Strategies for the Study of World Politics', *Millennium: Journal of International Studies* 39, no. 3 (2011): 781–803; and Meera Sabaratnam, 'Avatars of Eurocentrism in the Critique of the Liberal Peace', *Security Dialogue* 44, no. 3 (2013): 259–78.

discursive and non-discursive practices that straddle peacemaking and peacekeeping work within a broader context of enduring coloniality. Decolonial peacebuilding practices should therefore be aimed at effecting structural and institutional change; conflict prevention and protection; justice and healing; development and capacity-building; and governmental and multilateral humanitarian efforts that respect the agency of those most affected.

In the next three sections, I structure the argument around metageographies, masks or *Menschen* (human beings) and mundane matter as co-constitutive pillars, showing how a decolonial-feminist lens can change the way we look at gendered peacebuilding spaces, identities, infrastructures and the everyday, respectively. Firstly, metageographies draw attention to the gendered peace constructions that drive the feminisation of subjected regions and people – Africa in particular. Secondly, moving from the metatheoretical to the more tangible, masks or *Menschen* problematise human agency by looking at the 'alternative accounts of subjecthood'[9] expressed by all the stakeholders of the peacebuilding enterprise, both locally and internationally. With regard to the third pillar on matter, I make a case for considering the political economy of everyday (in)security and peacebuilding in conjunction with other materialities emanating from 'things', such as peace and security infrastructure. I argue that together these pillars constitute an integrated decolonised feminist frame for peacebuilding in an African context. In the final section, I introduce the notion of a feminist frontier to capture the integration of the three themes as well as what it means for moving the debate forward. The choice of the term 'frontier' is deliberate; I juxtapose it with the traditional understanding of frontier women in the West civilising the 'outback'. I theorise about the implications of intermediate spaces (borderlands) – those spaces between the three pillars – for a reconstituted gender–peacebuilding nexus. These liminal spaces offer ground(s) for reconsidering subjectivity in terms of epistemological, human and post-human shapes, from where I explore the value of 'feminist frontier' subjectivity as a critical tool for context-specific application in post-conflict spaces.

The unbearable coloniality of the gendered and racialised peace

Sabaratnam argues that critiques of the liberal peace, useful as they might be, have 'largely failed to dislodge the liberal peace as the central subject of inquiry' as a result of neoliberal governance becoming more politically correct and critics failing to come up with alternatives that are decolonial at their core.[10] And I would add that a concern for the everyday[11] and the local may have reproduced, albeit unintentionally, a sanitised picture of the local/traditional as gender-neutral and depoliticised, where chiefs still speak on behalf of rural women and other marginalised. Moreover, I contend, everyday peacebuilding and empathy/care principles are held up as 'new and progressive' directions, with little – if any – acknowledgement of the contribution of a maturing feminist body of scholarship on the ethics of care and the everyday of war and peace as personal and political.[12] I therefore share Vivienne Jabri's concern for the re-politicisation of peacebuilding. Her postcolonial analysis of the

---

[9]Sabaratnam, 'IR in Dialogue', 785.

[10]Ibid., 796–7; Sabaratnam, 'Avatars of Eurocentrism', 259–60.

[11]Oliver P. Richmond, 'A Post-Liberal Peace: Eirinism and the Everyday', *Review of International Studies* 35, no. 3 (2009): 557–80.

[12]Fiona Robinson, *The Ethics of Care: A Feminist Approach to Human Security* (Philadelphia: Temple University Press, 2011); Kate Bedford and Shirin M. Rai, 'Feminists Theorize International Political Economy', *Signs* 36, no. 1 (2010): 1–18; and Christine Sylvester, ed., *Experiencing War* (London: Routledge, 2011).

hegemonic status of peacebuilding reveals an important distinction 'between practices that view their target as populations to be governed and practices that recognise these populations and their conflicts as distinctly political'.[13] This colonial rationality to control people (whether through unilateralism or through hybridised/cooperative arrangements) stands in sharp contrast to decolonial or postcolonial approaches that recognise the political agency of the local actors.

Feminist critics of the liberal peace have concentrated on the oppressive ways in which the liberal peace project uses liberal-inspired gender discourses of gender equality to help enforce its norms and inform its practices on the ground.[14] The symbiotic relation between the liberal peace and a peace shaped by liberal feminism has led to a situation in practice where liberalism has become so embedded within mainstream discourses about gender and peacebuilding that it is very difficult to challenge – especially since this goes against the grain of widely held assumptions about gender mainstreaming on the basis of equal opportunities. And since liberal-feminist approaches as a rule do not see gender issues within a broader context of oppression, and consequently do not view gender as a product of, and productive of security practices, power structures are left untransformed.[15]

Feminist (mainly poststructuralist) critiques have therefore not succeeded in dislodging the liberal-feminist stranglehold over peacebuilding. For instance, much of the Foucauldian feminist work on gender and governmentality – although instructive – has drawn their critiques from largely Western roots. Thus, in order to disrupt this state of affairs, it would therefore be more appropriate to analyse liberal and post-liberal peacebuilding in the context of how it fits into an entangled global coloniality that is at once racialised, patriarchal, hetero-normative, Christian-centric, Euro or North American-centric, imperial, colonial and capitalist.[16] Viewed from this perspective, a gendered peace therefore forms part of the entanglement of multiple heterogeneous global hierarchies and hetararchies of sexual, linguistic and racial identities.

The proponents of decoloniality have argued that coloniality is a useful frame to rethink the basic premises of dependency and world-system theory;[17] along the lines of the colonial matrix of power, i.e. the coloniality of power, knowledge and being;[18] and as the 'darker side' of modernity.[19] María Lugones extends Quijano's coloniality of power to include the coloniality of gender.[20] These perspectives are suspicious of other critical theories, such as Marxism and Postcolonialism, which, they contend, have a different (Eurocentric) genealogy of thought, and which make it therefore difficult to disentangle the theory from the coloniality embedded in its analytical tools.[21] The kind of critical theory required to decolonise

---

[13]Vivienne Jabri, 'Peacebuilding, the Local and the International: A Colonial or Postcolonial Rationality?' *Peacebuilding* 1, no. 1 (2013): 6.

[14]See note 4.

[15]Amalia Sa'ar, 'Postcolonial Feminism, the Politics of Identification, and the Liberal Bargain', *Gender and Society* 19, no. 5 (2005): 689.

[16]Sabelo Ndlovu-Gatsheni, 'Global Coloniality and the Challenges of Creating African Futures', *Strategic Review for Southern Africa* 36, no. 2 (2014): 187–88.

[17]Ramón Grosfoguel, 'The Epistemic Decolonial Turn. Beyond Political-Economy Paradigms', *Cultural Studies* 21, no. 2–3 (2007): 211–23.

[18]Aníbal Quijano, 'Coloniality and Modernity', *Cultural Studies* 21, no. 2–3 (2007): 168–78.

[19]Walter D. Mignolo, *The Darker Side of Western Modernity: Decolonial Options* (Durham: Duke University Press, 2011).

[20]Lugones, 'Coloniality of Gender'.

[21]Mignolo, 'Coloniality of Power', 163–64; and Madina V. Tlostanova and Walter D. Mignolo, 'Global Coloniality and the Decolonial Option', *Kult* 6 (2009): 141–42.

cannot be one that stems from the West – it has to be one that originates from its margins or borders, where the oppression is felt. As Mignolo argues, 'colonial legacies experienced in the colonies are not part of the life and death of postmodern and poststructuralist theoreticians'.[22] So while a Western intellectual may be able to sense how coloniality works at a rational or intellectual level, he/she will find it hard to understand it at an experiential level.

Decolonial theory is therefore held up as a more authentic indigenous alternative for interpreting ambiguous and sharply polarised narratives and practices of Self–Other relations in the 'postcolony'. Mignolo explains that there are alternative ways of thinking and doing, originating in the developing world, that renegotiate not only the terms of the conversation but also the content away from a universalising 'theological (Renaissance) and egological (Enlightenment) politics of knowledge'.[23] It means that attempts to overcome the international–local dichotomy of liberal peacebuilding through the notion of 'liberal-local hybridity'[24] would therefore not shift the terms of the engagement far enough, as such a postcolonial critique remains lodged within a Eurocentric frame of thinking.

While I agree that there is always room for postcolonial analytics to be further decolonised,[25] I do not consider engaging in camp politics (alluded above) as helpful in the promotion of a decolonial agenda. I find the notion of coloniality useful to frame the problem at a global scale, but am wary that the notion of a stark remedy such as 'African solutions to African problems' could lead to the territorialisation or provincialisation of the production of peacebuilding knowledge. That said, a strategy of invoking 'colonial difference' to elevate sameness (often in terms of race) of a marginalised group to foster a shared identity for purposes of achieving a political goal is necessary in the context of global coloniality. Spivak's notion of 'strategic essentialism' is about using the concept of 'essence' critically, debating and contesting issues of group identity within the group.[26]

The flaws of postcolonialism are not necessarily transferable as is to postcolonial feminism. Postcolonial feminists (not feminist postcolonialists), in terms of decolonial credentials, have moved beyond a singular focus on race to include gender and other intersecting identities; equally they have acknowledged that, contrary to the broader feminist project that foregrounds gender, in colonised contexts, gender is often not the most important concern. In my view, even critics of the critics of liberal peace do not give enough credit to feminist work that is already decolonially troubling the international.[27] African gender research, for instance, seamlessly integrates decolonial and postcolonial approaches.[28] This body of research coheres around a common agenda of placing scholarship within historical contexts, attentive to its connection with broader political struggles. If peacebuilding is about addressing root causes, then an African postcolonial-feminist approach would seek to address the triad of gendered nationalisms, gendered militarisms and a violent postcolonial state as root causes while engaging in peacebuilding practices such as linking women's

---

[22]Walter D. Mignolo, 'Geopolitics of Sensing and Knowing on (De)coloniality, Border Thinking, and Epistemic Disobedience', *Postcolonial Studies* 14, no. 3 (2011): 280.

[23]Ibid., 274.

[24]Oliver P. Richmond, 'A Genealogy of Peace and Conflict Theory', in *Advances in Peacebuilding*, ed. Oliver P. Richmond (London: Palgrave, 2010), 14–38.

[25]Sabaratnam, 'Avatars of Eurocentrism', 260.

[26]Gayatri Chakravorty Spivak, *The Post-colonial Critic: Interviews, Strategies, Dialogues* (New York: Routledge, 1990).

[27]See seminal postcolonial-feminist works, such as Chandra Talpade Mohanty, '"Under Western Eyes" Revisited: Feminist Scholarship through Anticapitalist Struggles', *Signs: Journal of Women in Culture and Society* 28, no. 2 (2003): 499–535; and Vivienne Jabri, *The Postcolonial Subject. Claiming Politics/Governing Others in Late Modernity* (London: Routledge, 2013).

[28]Amina Mama, *Beyond the Masks: Race, Gender and Subjectivity* (New York: Routledge, 1995).

(reproductive) labour to everyday life, a gendered political economy and global coloniality. In view of such integrated treatment, I therefore prefer a broader framing of decoloniality that draws on elements of both decolonial and postcolonial feminist epistemologies.

Thus, the first pillar for developing a decolonising feminist approach to the gender–peacebuilding nexus is becoming aware of the gendered ways in which the West has been constructed as the primary subject of world peace and global security, and how the 'Rest', even when attention is on them, remains objectified and feminised. I term this 'metageographies'.

Metageographies and the construction of an African gendered nowhere

Drawing on feminist work that highlights the importance of the locus of production of gendered theory, I argue that gender and peacebuilding discourses are 'never without geography nor geographically innocent'.[29] I turn to Africa as a space, both metaphorically speaking and real. I use the term 'metageographies' to refer to those ideological mental-space constructions that help to entrench certain dominant peace, security and political economy discourses, policies and practices in Africa, ranging from post-conflict despair to the 'Africa Rising' hype. I therefore seek to problematise a singular 'totalizing spatial framework'[30] as one part of an integrated feminist frame for a more equitable gender and peacebuilding approach.

The colonisation of physical space through cartography, conquest and settlement continues when large-scale spatial constructs – combined with economic influence and an expansionist agenda (of the major powers) – act as drivers of particular worldviews (as we have seen in the case of the (neo)liberal peace), universalising their knowledge at the expense of 'lesser' regions and peoples. The counternarrative of the decolonial project maintains that Western perspectives on 'Africa' often disrespect the varieties of dynamics which tend to be lumped together 'into a core set of deficiencies' in an attempt to impose a rigid and stable order.[31] Reductionist representations depict Africa as one country; different, i.e. exotic; local, experiential and therefore outside the realm of theory-making; and as having history only in relation to Europe. It follows that Africa's marginalisation is complex. In this regard, Valentin Mudimbe reminds us Africa becomes an invention, not just in a geographic sense, but also in a metaphorical or ideological, and I would add, experiential, sense.[32]

But often this violent reproduction of Africa as 'the Other' comes in subtle Afro-optimist forms that make it so much harder to dislodge and for which the current analytical tools fall short. A case in point is the hype about 'Africa Rising'.[33] This discourse is fuelled by claims that 6 out of the world's 10 fastest growing economies during the period 2001–2010 were in Africa. Foreign direct investment is on a rapid upward trajectory and has since 2006 exceeded aid flows. Morten Jerven however questions the way in which African economic

---

[29] Janet Conway, 'Geographies of Transnational Feminisms: The Politics of Place and Scale in the World March of Women', *Social Politics* 15, no. 2 (2008): 224.

[30] Martin W. Lewis and Kären E. Wigen, *The Myth of Continents. A Critique of Metageography* (Los Angeles: University of California Press, 1997), 11.

[31] Jyotirmaya Tripathy and Dharmabrata Mohapatra, 'Does Development Exist outside Representation?' *Journal of Developing Societies* 27, no. 2 (2011): 114.

[32] Valentin Y. Mudimbe, *The Invention of Africa. Gnosis, Philosophy, and the Order of Knowledge* (Oxford: James Currey, 1988), 27.

[33] Christine Lagarde, 'Africa Rising – Building to the Future', Keynote Address, Maputo, May 29, 2014; also see the covers of *Time Magazine* (December 2012), *The Economist* (January 2013) and *The Official NEPAD Yearbook* for 2014.

development statistics are being produced and used, thereby exposing the limitations of our analytical tools.[34] The hype succeeds in diverting attention from the realities of massive inequality and poverty, violent conflict and pervasive sexual and gender-based violence (SGBV). When it comes to the governance of peacebuilding, the same picture emerges, with the 'emerging' powers (e.g. India, Brazil, South Africa and Turkey) cautiously proceeding to avoid harming their own economic growth and developmental agendas rather than making reform of the peace and security system a high priority.[35] This state of affairs may also indirectly explain the omission of gender from Sustainable Development Goal 16 on Peace, Justice and Sustainable Development. While it is encouraging that Goal 5 is devoted to gender equality and women's empowerment, the gender silences in Goal 16 are linked to a pragmatic consensus within the General Assembly to not let mandates overlap.[36] Sabelo Ndlovu-Gatsheni takes issue with the African players' uncritical adoption of such problem-solving narratives – 'for the AU to realise its [very ambitious] Agenda 2063 it has to struggle ceaselessly against global coloniality'.[37] He warns of the danger of reproducing a new form of dependency and scramble for resources by turning Africa's attention East.

It remains a delicate postcolonial balancing act for the AU to utilise the full peacebuilding potential of an innovative peace and security 'architecture' (e.g. Panel of the Wise) while stubbornly adhering to the solidarity norm. One of the dark sides of this practice – where African leaders engage in 'we-ness' and compromise in order not to upset a broad continental consensus[38] – is selective public and institutional support of the emerging continental gender equality regime.

The AU declared the years 2010–2020 to be the 'Women's Decade' and the AU theme for 2015 was also 'Women's Empowerment and Development towards the Implementation of Agenda 2063'. The text of Agenda 2063, launched in 2013, emphasises the empowerment of African women.[39] Yet, women are mostly referenced in tandem with youth (as if they share the same needs); in relation to development (Aspiration 6); and singled out as drivers of social change (Aspiration 5 on building a strong cultural identity, heritage and ethics), reinforcing stereotypes of women as carriers of culture and peace. There is thus very little in this document that challenges the coloniality of gender, and it indirectly contributes to the distanciation of government and legitimacy that comes with a focus on the governing of populations.[40]

Such gendered peacebuilding practices include, among others, integrating women into the security sector, but failing to fundamentally shift masculinist and militarist attitudes

---

[34]Morten Jerven, *Poor Numbers. How We are Misled by African Development Statistics and What To Do About It* (New York: Cornell University Press, 2013).

[35]Benjamin de Carvalho and Cedric de Coning, 'Rising Powers and the Future of Peacekeeping and Peacebuilding', *NOREF Norwegian Peacebuilding Resource Centre Report*, November 2013, http://peacebuilding.no/Themes/Emerging-powers/ Publications/Rising-powers-and-the-future-of-peacekeeping-and-peacebuilding (accessed September 2, 2015).

[36]https://sustainabledevelopment.un.org/sdgs (accessed January 6, 2016); Susan Hutchinson, 'Engendering Goal 16: Peace, Justice and Sustainable Development' (paper presented at the workshop on "Gender-Responsive Peacebuilding Post-2015: Concepts, Criticisms and Challenges", University of New South Wales, Sydney, November 23, 2015).

[37]Ndlovu-Gatsheni, 'Global Coloniality', 183.

[38]Thomas Kwasi Tieku, 'Theoretical Approaches to Africa's International Relations', in *Handbook of Africa's International Relations*, ed. Tim Murithi (London: Routledge), 16.

[39]African Union, 'Agenda 2063. The Africa We Want', 3rd ed., January 2015, http://www.adeanet.org/portalv2/en/system/files/ resources/01_agenda2063_popular_version_engs.pdf (accessed September 12, 2015).

[40]Jabri, 'Peacebuilding, the Local and the International', 12.

through human rights and gender awareness training. A case in point is the Southern African region where the Southern African Development Community (SADC) Protocol Barometer 2015 reports that there has been a vast improvement in the provision of sex-disaggregated data on security and a rise in the number of women included in security sector institutions. At 29%, Zimbabwe and Namibia included the highest proportion of women on peacekeeping missions in 2014. Yet, the institutions remain state-centric and human security issues do not receive any systematic attention.[41] Security Sector Reform (SSR) also serves as a good example of how discursive logic informs the situation on the ground in a hegemonic way. The cyclical logic that security needs development and development needs security has informed SSR in general as well as its gendered practices. Because gender inequality is considered detrimental to development and violence against women seen as a form of insecurity with negative consequences for development, this 'logic' now dictates the dominant view of regarding SSR as a key element in the long-term prevention of SGBV. [42]

The coloniality of power is further masked by the fact that Africa is a lively testing ground for approaches to address gender inequality and insecurity, such as the adoption of numerous UNSC Resolutions on WPS (e.g. 1325, 1820, 1960, 2122 and 2242 as well as National Action Plans to facilitate the implementation of Resolution 1325). But it leaves the coloniality of knowledge unchanged. Women's multidimensional insecurity and gender as a cross-cutting issue are foregrounded to reinforce the empirical significance of the continent at the expense of its theoretical agency. This collusion between gender equality myths and African myths reinforces the impression that the continent is an empirical site where interesting or deviant things happen and which shape practical knowledge only. The result is that Africa is feminised and its marginalisation reinforced, relegating both women and Africa to the private (empirical/experiential) sphere leaving Africa and its deeper gender questions everywhere but nowhere.[43]

Of masks and *Menschen*

In this section, I argue that taking the presence of subjects in peacebuilding seriously is a fundamental decolonial act. 'Masks' signifies the epistemological need to expose what lies beneath stereotypes of what constitutes the human dimension, what it means to be a *Mensch* (German for human being, or *mentsh* in Yiddish, colloquially meaning a person of integrity and honour). The seemingly neutral meaning of *Mensch* (denoting the average human being, flawed but well-intentioned most of the time) and the positive connotation of *mentsh* belie the reality of gendered power dynamics among peacebuilders on the ground. Between *Mensch* (ironically masculine in the German language) and *Unmensch*, we find a whole spectrum of characters, whether colonial masters, liberal peacebuilders seeing themselves as messiahs, muggers/warlords posing as good 'guys', mothers or just men. What they

---

[41]See Chapter 8 of Colleen Lowe Morna, Sifiso Dube and Lucia Makamure, eds., *SADC Gender Protocol Barometer 2015*, Johannesburg: Gender Links. http://www.genderlinks.org.za/article/sadc-gender-protocol-barometer-2015-2015-07-16 (accessed January 6, 2016), 275, 289.

[42]Heidi Hudson, 'Untangling the Gendering of the Security-Development Nexus', in *Handbook of International Security and Development*, ed. Paul Jackson (Cheltenham: Edward Elgar, 2015), 51–2.

[43]Heidi Hudson, 'Subversion of an Ordinary Kind: Gender, Security and Everyday', in *Africa in Global International Relations. Emerging Approaches to Theory and practice*, eds. Paul-Henri Bischoff, Kwesi Aning and Amitav Acharya (London: Routledge, 2016), 43–63.

share is their humanity or lack thereof, and varying levels of human subjectivity. For the subaltern, agency is the ability to resist oppression; for the liberal 'Self', it may very well be the ability to step back because as Jabri argues, agency is 'at once enabled and constrained by the structural continuities of the international'.[44]

But should we not abandon the notion of agency for its perceived Western roots, stemming from a liberal fixation on individualism and the 'right' to have choices and the ability to act on them? I argue not, provided the concept is 'troubled'. Individualist tenets are somewhat softened if we consider evidence of collective agency, the type that builds transnational feminist solidarity or Pan-Africanism as a strategy to express Afrocentric agency.[45] From this we can deduce that agency and human subjectivity are always socially situated (relational), structurally embedded and historically shaped. Context therefore matters in terms of how much agency peacebuilding actors in Africa are able to enact within a global coloniality. Constraints on agency become evident when male and female subjects are confined to static and homogeneous categories, typecasting men as protectors and/or aggressors and women as peaceful mothers. If liberal discourses work with a binary of femininity vs. masculinity, women are cast as victims, immediately reinforcing the positive masculinity (protector) and negative masculinity (perpetrator) of men.[46] With such strong gendered stereotypes in action, it means that women are assumed to have no agency, and if they do, the only way to explain when they transgress the norms of femininity is by depicting them as deviants, as in Rwanda.[47] In Rwanda, leading the world in terms of women's parliamentary representation with 64% in 2015,[48] also, women were 'allowed' to enter politics en masse on the basis that as mothers they are innately more peaceful and less corrupt.

Therefore what matters for the decolonial project is to 'trouble' these binaries by looking at 'how agency is constructed and assigned/denied by others, ... who are operating off of (mis)perceptions and assumptions'.[49] In this regard, Jessica Auchter criticises the way feminists inscribe agency into women's narratives without asking 'what this means and what emancipation and agency are linked to' and in the process reproducing oppression.[50] She argues that we should stop fixating on agency, and rather try to understand the actions themselves. Letting the actions speak for themselves could possibly be the ultimate act of agency. It means that before we begin to look at categories of peacebuilding agents, we need to trouble the notion of agency itself. As the discussion about masculinity vs. femininity above suggests, orthodox peacebuilding practice presents us with only two choices – agent or non-agent/victim,[51] couched in normative terms as a binary between agency as good and victimhood as bad. The practice of gendering peacebuilding, e.g. SSR, does however

---

[44]Jabri, 'Peacebuilding, the Local and the International', 10.

[45]Molefi K. Asante, *Afrocentricity: The Theory of Social Change* (Chicago: African American Images, 2003).

[46]Hudson, 'Double-edged Sword of Peace', 450.

[47]Sara E. Brown, 'Female Perpetrators of the Rwandan Genocide', *International Feminist Journal of Politics* 16, no. 3 (2014): 460.

[48]The World Bank, 'Proportion of Seats Held by Women in National Parliaments', http://data.worldbank.org/indicator/SG.GEN. PARL.ZS (accessed January 3, 2016).

[49]Caron E. Gentry, 'Thinking about Women, Violence, and Agency', *International Feminist Journal of Politics* 14, no. 1 (2012): 80.

[50]Ibid., 81; Caron Gentry commenting in her introduction of the *International Feminist Journal of Politics* article cluster 'Thinking about Women, Violence and Agency' on Jessica Auchter's contribution.

[51]Jessica Auchter, 'Gendering Terror: Discourses of Terrorism and Writing', *International Feminist Journal of Politics* 14, no. 1 (2012): 123.

reveal nuances, such as 'good' victims or 'bad' agents when women's organisations take their watchdog role too seriously.[52]

Another dimension of decolonising the human subject is to use intersectionality as a critical feminist lens to study multiple manifestations of agency.[53] Among gender-blind and gender-aware (read: women) approaches to peacebuilding, we now also see so-called 'gender-relational' approaches emerging that recognise the absence of sexual and gender minorities, including intersex, transgender and third gender persons, and masculinities from peacebuilding discourse, programmes and policies.[54] The latter approach – couched in terms that policy-makers and practitioners can digest – comes closest to the radical decolonial feminist option of intersectionality, which is different from an additive approach that ends up reifying identity politics. In contrast, this approach considers raced, classed, gendered, sexualised, national, ethnic, cultural and religious identities and oppressions as interdependent. A focus on the intersection serves to unmask and destabilise hierarchies of oppressions that hide inequalities within as well as across categories. Lugones observes in this regard that '[i]t is only when we perceive gender and race as intermeshed or fused that we actually see women of color'.[55] Once we see what is missing, the logic of the connections has to be rethought. From the synthesis sometimes emerges a transformed idea of 'what is regarded to be a feminist issue and what is included as gendered experience'.[56]

Thus, since what we see determines what we fund, this gender tool is crucial in devising a truly decolonised system of resource distribution. In the policy world of peacebuilding, the allocation of resources for Disarmament, Demobilisation and Reintegration remains skewed in favour of male combatants.[57] Consequently, within an additive model, marginal groups are forced to compete against one another for resources, which helps little in moving groups out of their marginal status. Sometimes both gender- and race-targeted policies fail to meet the needs of groups because planners were unaware or overlooked the complexities emanating from an interface of multiple identities. For that matter, analysis of the identities of the international donor community (the so-called 'messiahs' or 'masters') complements a consideration of the many faces of the so-called 'muggers' at the local level – challenging the contention of some scholars[58] that critics of the liberal peace focus too much on the agency and subjecthood of interveners.

A more nuanced, inclusive and relational analysis of agency reveals, for instance, the ambivalent power relations between women's organisations and donors and how the campaign against SGBV has been 'marketised'. Évelyne Jean-Bouchard shows how women's organisations in Eastern Democratic Republic of Congo (DRC) utilise SGBV discourses to gain visibility for themselves in international fora. Donor funding also brings legitimacy

---

[52]Hudson, 'Double-edged Sword of Peace', 450–1.

[53]Kimberlé Crenshaw, 'Mapping the Margins: Intersectionality, Identity Politics and Violence Against Women of Color', *Stanford Law Review* 43, no. 6 (1991): 1241–99.

[54]Catalina Rojas, 'Gender and Peacebuilding Resource Guide', *Peace and Collaborative Development Network*, March 8, 2015, http://www.internationalpeaceandconflict.org/profiles/blogs/guide-to-gender-and-peacebuilding#.VfRi7WUaKM8 (accessed September 2, 2015); Henri Myrttinen, Jana Naujoks and Judy El-Bushra, 'Rethinking Gender in Peacebuilding', *International Alert*, March 2014.

[55]Lugones, 'Coloniality of Gender', 4.

[56]Vivian M. May, 'Intellectual Genealogies, Intersectionality, and Anna Julia Cooper', in *Feminist Solidarity at the Crossroads. Intersectional Women's Studies for Transracial Alliance*, ed. Kim M. Vaz and Gary L. Lemons (New York: Routledge, 2012), 59.

[57]Megan H. MacKenzie, *Female Soldiers in Sierra Leone: Sex, Security, and Post-Conflict Development* (New York: New York University Press, 2012).

[58]Sabaratnam, 'Avatars of Eurocentrism', 264, 266.

for women to 'bargain' with traditional authorities. In order to preserve this new status, women then tend to emphasise the brutal nature of sexual violence and insist on preserving the image of the female rape victim. An intersectional lens subverts how we read agency because while this could be seen as a case of local–donor complicity, we should not overstate the inevitability of local ideological co-optation in Western peacebuilding initiatives. Local women's organisations have to negotiate between international norms and concrete local demands. As Deniz Kandiyoti[59] and Amalia Sa'ar[60] have shown, decisions by members of disadvantaged groups to internalise a liberal epistemology are influenced by the materiality and political economy of lived experience and social context. The legitimacy gained from their international association and donor funding to address sexual violence indirectly affords DRC women's NGOs the opportunity to draw attention to issues that may be more important to women than war-time rape, such as access to land, marriage and succession.[61] Such strategic choices and expressions of political agency must therefore be understood in the context of a wide range of active and passive strategies employed by marginalised people to maximise security and optimise life choices. This case also emphasises that an intersectional approach that treats overlapping identity categories as if they were all equal, will fail to decentre the liberal (Western) assumptions of much feminist activism currently.[62] Amidst an openness to diverse and intertwined identity connections, we nevertheless need to make sure that discussions of coloniality of power do not abstract from gender (in whatever form it presents itself), as this will risk re-inscribing gender binaries.[63]

The mundane really *matters*

While the notion of 'everyday peacebuilding'[64] is a step in the right direction, a specific recognition of the *gendered* nature of the everyday is crucial for elevating a postcolonial focus on local–global hybrid interaction around post-conflict reconstruction to a fundamentally transformed (decolonial) understanding of peacebuilding practices. Lugones states that the production of the everyday through food, economies, ecologies, symbols, space, time and clothing should not just be colonially different. They should include 'affirmation of life over profit, communalism over individualism, "estar" [to be] over enterprise, beings in relation rather than dichotomously split over and over in hierarchically and violently ordered fragments'.[65] With this in mind, the final pillar towards building a feminist frontier tilts the lens slightly away from human subjectivity to consider it in relation to non- or post-human subjectivities.[66] Decentring the human subject does not mean that humanity is jettisoned; it simply means human subjectivity loses its place of dominance and instead

---

[59]Deniz Kandiyoti, 'Bargaining with Patriarchy', *Gender & Society* 2, no. 3 (1988): 274–90.

[60]Sa'ar, 'Postcolonial Feminism', 680–700.

[61]Évelyne Jean-Bouchard, 'Sexual Violence Issues in Eastern Congo: Normative Processes of Local and Global Co-constitutions' (paper presented at the International Studies Association Conference, San Francisco, CA, April 3–6, 2013).

[62]Sara Salem, 'Decolonial Intersectionality and a Transnational Feminist Movement', 2014, http://thefeministwire.com/2014/04/decolonial-intersectionality/ (accessed April 22, 2014).

[63]Schiwy, 'Decolonization and Subjectivity', 275.

[64]Oliver P. Richmond, 'Resistance and the Post-liberal Peace', *Millennium: Journal of International Studies* 38, no. 3 (2010): 665–92.

[65]Lugones, 'Decolonial Feminism', 754.

[66]In *Reassembling the Social: An Introduction to Actor-Network-Theory* (Oxford: Oxford University Press, 2005), Bruno Latour ascribes agency to inanimate entities.

operates relationally within a post-anthropocentric future.[67] I argue for a decentring of the public human figure (liberal man), while advocating for bringing the private human (colonial woman, queer, etc.) back in. For feminist scholars, this is nothing new. I propose to do this through an analysis of some of the gendered and racialised material dimensions of lived, everyday peace and security, such as political economies of peacekeeping and private security infrastructural control.

Lived experiences are the sites where interlocked identities manifest. It is also through these experiences that categories can be subverted. As Fierke remarks, '[such] embodied security is … fundamentally bound up in the interaction between humans and their material environment'.[68] In the same way that war is a sensed experience and a practice of the human body[69], so is peacebuilding. Mignolo too describes decolonising acts as epistemological acts that prioritise sensing and the body.[70] Peace is then not something that happens *to* people, but something that is embodied and felt. And because of that, a decolonial everyday peace cannot be universalised and has to have a geo-historical point of origin.[71]

Feminists[72] have argued that gender analysis offers a bottom-up foundational logic that, in the peacebuilding context, serves to counter the disempowering neglect of liberal peace-building of the agency and needs of civil society actors. The tendency to construct a binary between state and civil society (non-state) is a Western practice that masks huge dispar-ities in power that exist between different civil society actors (especially in the aftermath of conflict). When armed non-state actors' needs are met (e.g. rebels and warlords) and others not (e.g. children, women, the elderly and/or transgender), it risks reproducing a new kind of micro-coloniality. An intersectional lens is therefore also important to avoid conflict among groups. A bottom-up approach firstly underscores the need to develop a new vocabulary for bringing local, civil society understandings of everyday securitisation and the informal and hybrid forms of democracy and governance to the forefront. It compels us to consider the informality of peacebuilding and private security arrangements at the community level. In this way, the everyday as a source of 'empirical' theorising from below takes shape. Theory is made in the liminal space between geopolitics, macroeconomics and global terrorism, on the one hand, and the sharp end where ordinary people are affected by and negotiate global governance policies, on the other. And rather than simply inserting gender into peacebuilding discourse and practice, a more sustainable and decolonising approach would be to focus on how women's and men's everyday lives are affected by the complex relationship between gendered capitalist and militarist processes and how men and women negotiate their lives through both.[73] If peacebuilding and peacekeeping economies capture a large part of everyday life after conflict, such as domestic, sex and private security

---

[67]Rosi Braidotti, *The Posthuman* (Cambridge: Polity, 2013).

[68]Karin M. Fierke, 'Is There Life Beyond Language? Discourses of Security' (paper presented at the International Studies Association Conference, San Francisco, CA, April 3–6, 2013).

[69]Laura Sjoberg, *Gendering Global Conflict. Toward a Feminist Theory of War* (New York: Columbia University Press, 2013), 253.

[70]Mignolo, 'Geopolitics of Sensing', 273–83.

[71]See Sjoberg, *Gendering Global Conflict*, 268; and Mignolo, 'Geopolitcs of Sensing', 275.

[72]Georgina Waylen, 'You Still Don't Understand: Why Troubled Engagements Continue between Feminists and (critical) IPE', *Review of International Studies* 32 (2006), 153.

[73]Amina Mama and Margo Okazawa-Rey, 'Militarism, Conflict and Women's Activism in the Global Era: Challenges and Prospects for Women in Three West African Contexts', *Feminist Review* 101 (2012): 97–123.

work,[74] decolonial thinking about the political economy of peace interventions would be concerned with those people targeted by the intervention as well as the material effects of the intervention.[75] And for feminists, the gendered dimensions of how peace is produced on a daily basis always exist within the context of gender-skewed global processes.

Secondly, beyond the gendered and racialised day-to-day political economy interaction between locals and international peacekeepers, for instance, a bottom-up peacebuilding logic should include a consideration of other materialities. It 'pays' to problematise the material power of infrastructural assemblages that mask as peace infrastructures but are in fact forms of control and political ordering. For instance, in the DRC, there are distinct spatial concentrations of private security companies ensconced in compounds behind high walls and barbed wire, regulated by curfews and security checks, to protect mining interests and NGOs/aid workers. This phenomenon illustrates how infrastructural power acquires a life of its own, a kind of post-human agency[76] when it is used as a proxy for stabilisation or statebuilding.[77] What would decolonial everyday peacebuilding look like when confronted by the agency of things, in this case infrastructure? In sharp contrast with Lugones' everyday as one of harmony of beings and things, creating pockets of liberal governance where the Hobbesian state of nature is kept at bay has serious implications for the private–public dichotomy and the decolonial-feminist project of decentring the public. While the assertion of post-human agency may appear to disrupt the dominance of the public, this is not the case. In this instance, the alliance between state and private security providers is counterbalanced by the distance it creates between state and citizen, those existing on the racialised and gendered fringes, whose everyday security is dependent on the discourses and actions of the powerful. This so-called 'new public' where state and private actors cohabitate is still a public upon which the 'Other' is dependent. Privatisation of security through 'infrastructural' rule thus creates more inequality, erects more physical and mental boundaries and perpetuates coloniality.

It follows then that materialities of the everyday come in different shapes and have ambivalent implications for thinking about meaningful ways to broaden agency. Key to making sense of the human and non-human entanglement of peacebuilding practices is to become attentive to the multiple ways in which matter impacts the colonial, racialised, gendered, sexualised and capitalist difference that makes up the life worlds of the people the liberal peace is aimed at.[78]

Conclusion: Feminist frontiers taming the West or the Rest?

This article has drawn on a variety of material and discursive peacebuilding practices such as SSR, the campaign against SGBV, peacekeeping economies and private security. I have argued by means of three conceptual pillars – metageographies, masks and *Menschen*

---

[74]Kathleen M. Jennings, 'Service, Sex, and Security: Gendered Peacekeeping Economies in Liberia and the Democratic Republic of the Congo', *Security Dialogue* 45, no. 4 (2014): 313–30.

[75]Sabaratnam, 'Avatars of Eurocentrism', 273.

[76]e.g. Claudia Aradau, 'Security That Matters: Critical Infrastructure and Objects of Protection', *Security Dialogue* 41 (2010): 491–514; and William E. Connolly, 'The "New Materialism" and the Fragility of Things', *Millennium – Journal of International Studies* 41, no. 3 (2013): 399–412.

[77]Peer Schouten, 'The Materiality of State Failure: Social Contract Theory, Infrastructure and Governmental Power in Congo', *Millennium – Journal of International Studies* 41, no. 3 (2013): 573.

[78]Sabaratnam, 'IR in Dialogue', 799; Lugones, 'Decolonial Feminism', 746.

(human agency) and mundane matters (materiality) – that a critical decolonial gender lens allows us a deeper view of peacebuilding as a political project. It exposes the disempowering consequences for marginalised populations in post-conflict states by drawing attention to the way in which peace interventions engage in intertwined, gendered, racialised and sexualised forms of othering. With regard to the first pillar, feminists have successfully linked the social situatedness of knowledge in everyday life with inequalities in the global knowledge project. Liberal peace critics can learn from this. The challenge is not to insert Africa into global peace discourses, but to rethink the logic of relations, and from there finding an authentic African peacebuilding identity that is neither essentialist nor a proxy for liberal interests. A normative concern with positionality in these abstract metageographical spaces provides a foundation for the generation of radically different peacebuilding epistemologies. With regard to the second pillar, the introduction of alternative subjecthoods becomes necessary to challenge the narrowing and dehumanising effects of coloniality on peacebuilding practice. Through reading history differently, and seeing peacebuilding as political, the differentiation of actors becomes important,[79] because it reveals diverse but often concealed subjectivities. In this way, we can begin to rethink human agency as an essentially contentious practice rather than as something bestowed upon the locals by internationals. Critical feminist concepts such as intersectionality, combined with an explicit decolonial agenda, contribute towards recognising a variety of subjectivities, prompted and shaped by changing positionalities and locales. This human space is followed by the third pillar where humans have to renegotiate their position in relation to planetary concerns where matter and the materiality of living and experiencing peace in a sensory manner lead to a somewhat disturbing mix of conflict and cooperation. It involves respectful scholarship: treating human, lived experiences as legitimate and not as culturally deviant or exceptional. It also entails looking for clues of 'embryonic conversations' between human and post-human agency, to reunite what colonial alienation has schizophrenically pushed apart. As Ngũgĩ wa Thiong'o contends, 'an active (or passive) distancing of oneself from the reality around; and an active (or passive) identification with that which is most external to one's environment ... [has produced] a society of bodiless heads and headless bodies'.[80]

I deliberately employ the 'feminist frontiers' concept in a paradoxical way – a play on 'feminist vanguard' intent on transforming the world, critical of masculine space, white middle-class female privilege, and the freedom offered by frontiers such as globalisation, cyberspace and even transnational feminist spaces;[81] but also invoking the irony of the image of white frontier women civilising the West in an article on coloniality. Still, feminist frontiers connote being 'out there' – the opposite of the homeland, engaging the unknown, therefore a kind of border thinking alternative for peacebuilding.

Border thinking or epistemology is the decolonial response to the colonial difference.[82] It represents an alter-space where alternative knowledge is produced, where one 'affectively

---

[79]Jabri, 'Peacebuilding, the Local and the International', 15.
[80]Ngũgĩ wa Thiong'o, *Decolonising the Mind. The Politics of Language in African Literature* (London: James Currey, 1989).
[81]Anna M. Agathangelou and Heather M. Turcotte, '"Feminist" Theoretical Inquiries and "IR"', in *The International Studies Encyclopedia*, ed. Robert A. Denemark (2010), http://www.isacompendium.com/subscriber/uid=5662/tocnode?id=g9781444336597_yr2013_chunk_g97814443365978_ss1-12 (accessed December 1, 2014); Lynne Phillips, 'Genders, Spaces, Places', in *The International Studies Encyclopedia*, ed. Robert A. Denemark (2010), http://www.isacompendium.com/subscriber/uid=5662/tocnode?id=g9781444336597_yr2013_chunk_g97814443365979_ss1-10 (accessed December 1, 2014).
[82]Mignolo cited in Lugones, 'Decolonial Feminism', 753.

de-link[s] … from the imperial/colonial organization of society'.[83] Delinking is however not about isolation; it is about not accepting the negative peace options that are available and consistently challenging these. By bringing feminist theorising on the metageographical, human and post-human subjectivities into play, a new borderland space is created. The frontier is therefore not the border*line* or margin, but the in-between, the liminal, the borderlands. Unlike frontiers that are eventually absorbed into the main political authority through conventional peacebuilding, this borderland is global yet local. The space is inter-mediate – between the narrative construction of Africa and its everyday realities; between the overlapping identities that constitute the human condition; and between humans and a brave new (material) world. At the same time, the space is mediated because in all three thematic pillars, the relationality of subjectivity determines how the gendering of peace-building in Africa could become a decolonial response to the colonial difference.

Practically speaking, I would argue that the feminist frontier tool facilitates decolonial analysis post-conflict through context-specific, non-linear application of a combination of epistemological, ontological and ethnographic interventions. In Africa, for instance, one could begin by firstly drawing out the coloniality of a specific postcolonial post-conflict context and challenging one-dimensional metageographical inventions of 'Mother' Africa through more rounded feminist epistemologies of peace. Macro-feminist insights serve to frame the more particular analysis of human and non-human subjectivities in context but are also informed by the insights from below. Secondly, the roles and contested 'essences' of all human peacebuilding agents must be understood ontologically as intersected and gender-relational. Lastly, the governance and biopolitical roles of non-human agencies in that ontological context are foregrounded by centring private, everyday and other material peacebuilding practices.

I therefore view the concept of 'feminist frontiers' as a heuristic tool to bring the concep-tualisation of spaces and subjectivities in the three core areas together. The concept serves to guide the interpretation of polarised narratives of Self–Other relations as well as the ambiguous consequences of materialities in the postcolony. The concept is fluid, yet also stabilising. It wants to unite, but without suffocating diversity. That is why it is frontiers, not frontier. But it also marks a point of resistance and contestation in a space where things will be different but not necessarily always better (not an idealised space). In this sense, the frontier serves not only as a corrective to the hype about African futures, but also connects past oppressions with a future where Africa may be rising only for 'the few'. The feminist frontiers concept thus serves as a fulcrum around which a set of conceptual tools can be developed to offer more sober (and substantive) analyses of the present rather than relying on unhelpful and harmful dichotomised pasts and futures. The conceptual tool also offers the possibility of revisiting material delineations and consequences, showing how the material and the discursive dimensions of relations are co-constituted. Coloniality is everywhere. The challenge is to create a decolonial borderland that will eventually eclipse it.

Acknowledgements

I would like to thank the two reviewers as well as Kathleen Jennings for their helpful comments on drafts of this article.

---

[83]Tlostanova and Mignolo, 'Coloniality and the Decolonial Option', 132.

Disclosure statement

No potential conflict of interest was reported by the author.

Feminists building peace and reconciliation: beyond post-conflict

Elisabeth Porter

Centre for Peace & Security, Hawke Research Institute, University of South Australia, Adelaide, Australia

ABSTRACT
Many feminists find the concept of 'post-conflict' troubling for two main reasons. First, the discursive space of post-conflict is contestable with fuzzy lines around when the conflict period becomes post-conflict. Second, for women, the period following the cessation of armed aggression continues to be one of insecurity, where intimate partner violence often remains high, particularly when male ex-combatants return from fighting. In the so-called post-conflict period, a culture of gendered violence, gendered insecurity and militarisation remains. I argue that the transition from conflict provides opportunities for transformation from a culture of violence to one of peace, from insecurity to security and from antagonism to reconciliation. This article outlines a four-fold conceptualisation of reconciliation as a spectrum, reconciling relationships, processes and cultures of reconciliation. To move beyond gender-blind notions of post-conflict, the article seeks to decipher what is uniquely feminist about these ideas in affirming feminist peacebuilding and reconciliation.

Reconciliation is, understandably, seen as post-conflict work. However, for feminists, the concept of the 'post-conflict' is problematic.[1] There are two strong reasons why this is the case: the concept is ambiguous in obscuring the insecurities people experience after the cessation of war, ignoring the gender-specific ways that women and men experience insecurity and security; and it understates the degree to which gendered violence remains in a militarised or previously violent culture. The overall argument of this article is that the period of transition from violence towards sustainable peace provides peacebuilders with many opportunities to introduce transformative changes, including those brought about in meaningful reconciliation. Transforming relationships from domination and violence to cooperation and mutual respect is intrinsic to feminist politics. Transforming relationships that have been damaged by violent conflict into workable relationships also lies at the heart of reconciliation. Yet, while feminists have produced important scholarship on the problems associated with a lack of gender sensitivity in post-conflict peacebuilding, and on the harms of gender-based violence, less feminist work appears specifically on reconciliation.[2]

---

[1] As is custom, I will no longer put post-conflict in quotation marks, given that the paper is problematising its usage.
[2] I explain later that women write on truth and reconciliation commissions and some men write on the impact of reconciliation for women, but scholarship on reconciliation from an explicitly feminist perspective is rare.

This article critically explores peacebuilding and reconciliation with a view to explaining what unique contribution feminists can make to moving practices beyond gender-blind post-conflict mindsets.

This article has three sections. The first section scrutinises the idea of the post-conflict, its ambiguity and prevailing gendered violence. The reason to stress this lingering violence is that few reconciliation theorists heed it, viewing reconciliation as primarily something that occurs between former warring political actors. I am arguing that the transformative opportunities inherent in reconciliatory spaces can flow throughout all social and political levels in everyday practices. Hence, groundwork is first needed to set the scene for why a culture of gendered violence stultifies not only a progression of peace, but also the practical outworking of reconciliation. The second section canvases literature around reconciliation understood in a four-fold way as a spectrum, relationships, processes and cultures. Literature used in this section is not explicitly feminist. However, it highlights the potential in which feminists can work further to open spaces in which reconciliation might be possible. The third section briefly draws out what is a uniquely feminist contribution to building reconciliation. This contribution moves the scholarly discussion into concrete everyday practices. In this post-war space, feminists have a lot to offer in showing how empathy and truth-telling can play significant personal and political roles in facilitating the conditions in which reconciliation might occur.

Fuzzy, insecure and violent post-conflict periods

The concept of post-conflict has 'contested temporal and spatial aspects' with fuzzy lines between where conflict ends and post-conflict begins.[3] The way that post-conflict is understood has impact on gender security. Hence, this ambiguity about the start and end points of post-conflict needs to be unpacked, as well as an understanding of why gendered violence remains.

Ambiguity between conflict and post-conflict

Certainly ceasefires are significant in heralding a welcome change, but rarely is there a clear moment when violence conclusively ends and peace begins. Peacebuilding occurs while conflict is raging, dying down, flares up, coincides with a ceasefire and continues towards stable peace. Flux, renegotiation of roles and power plays are affected by the type of gender relations that existed prior to and during the conflict, but these relations become potentially more open in the sociopolitical space when armed conflict really has ceased. On the continuum between conflict, negotiations, peacekeeping, humanitarian aid, peacebuilding and reconstruction, the re-construction dimension must be interrogated also, because rarely does it remove all forms of gender injustice, inequality and exclusion that contribute to the generation of conflict.[4] That is, with those conducting the negotiating and making decisions, there is a tendency to use peace negotiations as leverage for reintroducing the

---

[3]Laura McLeod, 'Configurations of Post-conflict: Impacts of Representations of Conflict and Post-conflict upon the (Political) Translations of Gender Security within UNSCR 1325', *International Feminist Journal of Politics* 13, no. 4 (2011): 595.
[4]See Marcia E. Greenberg and Elaine Zuckerman, 'The Gender Dimension of Post-Conflict Reconstruction: The Challenges in Development Aid', in *Making Peace Work: The Challenges of Social and Economic Reconstruction*, ed. Tony Addison and Tilman Brück (London: Palgrave MacMillan, 2009). Rather than reconstruction, these authors stress peace, participation and prosperity.

BUILDING PEACE

pre-war stability that is tantamount to reinstating the old powerful order. Women, rarely part of the pre-war hierarchy, are usually excluded from the post-war processes, despite many having gained considerable expertise in local grass roots peacebuilding.[5]

The absence of war does not indicate peace, particularly where security is militarised. When women are asked about what they fear and what makes them feel safe, generally, they refer to personal needs in the home, street, neighbourhood, village or refugee camp. In truth commissions in particular, they tend to speak about what happened to their male relatives, and when they do speak of their own trauma, their stories are situated within their everyday experiences.[6] The significance of this extends beyond truth commissions. It signals that the everyday local site constitutes a culturally appropriate configuration of individual and community 'life and care'.[7] Of course this everyday life affects men and women, but attention to differences is important. In the everyday routine of women and girls, there is often a serious disconnect 'between security and well-being'.[8] In 2000, the United Nation High Commissioner of Refugees no longer had funds to purchase soap for a half a million refugees in Tanzania. Consequently, the girls dropped out of school and incidents of girls having sex in exchange for soap increased. Soap, an everyday item, proved not only essential for personal hygiene, but for the girls' protection.[9] Few would consider soap to be a significant gender concern in influencing post-conflict needs, but this example shows why it is. It is part of what authors call 'social services justice' which can assist the realisation of gender centrality in two ways; this justice responds to everyday daily needs, and it expands the emphasis of justice to embrace basic material needs for victims.[10] In 'grounding post-conflict needs in lived experiences', a gender-sensitive response to insecurities is more likely.[11]

The need to make gender central arises because while sometimes women and men share insecurities, other times different vulnerabilities occur. Consequently, there are gender-specific requirements needed in the aftermath of violence. Hence, a project such as disarmament, demobilisation and reintegration (DDR) will have explicit gender dimensions in the type of trauma counsel needed, as well as the kind of retraining and economic skills desired for successful reintegration of former female and male combatants. Regarding insecurities, simplistic dichotomies that assume all men are perpetrators of brutality and all women are victims of abuse fail to consider some men's vulnerabilities to violence, including sexual assault as part of torture, and women's reproduction of violence either through traditional socialisation of boys or as female combatants.

Nevertheless, there is sufficient evidence that sexual violence against women tends to increase at the end of war.[12] Research shows that in the period deemed to be post-conflict, violence against women often 'increases beyond pre-war levels and sometimes even beyond

---

[5]Tarja Väyrynen reminds us that international peacebuilders and 'local subaltern subjects' have dissimilar understandings of the post-conflict situation and of 'gendered agency' in 'Gender and Peacebuilding', in *Palgrave Advances in Peacebuilding: Critical Developments and Approaches*, ed. Oliver P. Richmond (New York: Palgrave MacMillan, 2010), 151.

[6]See Fiona Ross, 'An Acknowledged Failure: Women, Voice, Violence, and the South African Truth and Reconciliation Commission', in *Localizing Transitional Justice: Interventions and Priorities after Mass Violence*, ed. Rosalind Shaw and Lars Waldorf (Stanford, CA: Stanford University Press, 2010), 69–91.

[7]Oliver Richmond, 'A Post-liberal Peace: Eirenism and the Everyday', *Review of International Studies* 35, no. 2 (2009): 561.

[8]Nadine Puechguirbal, 'The Cost of Ignoring Gender in Conflict and Post-conflict Situations: A Feminist Perspective', *Amsterdam Law Forum* 4, no. 1 (2012): 13.

[9]Ibid.

[10]Naomi Cahn, Dina Haynes and Fionnuala Ní Aoláin, 'Returning Home: Women in Post-conflict Societies', *Baltimore Law Review* 39 (2009–2010): 339–69.

[11]Ibid., 341–42.

[12]Jacqui True, *The Political Economy of Violence against Women* (New York: Oxford University Press, 2012).

wartime levels', particularly when the partner is a former combatant.[13] Indeed, even women who were active in liberation struggles such as in Algeria, Eritrea, Mozambique, Namibia, Vietnam and Zimbabwe 'experience a backlash in their relations with men', and often are forced back into the kitchen or fields.[14] The limitations of pre-existing cultural norms of women's economic dependency are 'exacerbated by political conflict', preventing women from being able to leave violent men.[15] There are connections between intimate partner violence and the gendered violence that is manifest during armed conflict.[16] These connections between private and public acts of violence by combatants, former combatants and (generally speaking) other men constitute a 'web of harms',[17] with intersecting 'continuities of violence for women'.[18]

In both intimate partner violence and war-rape, the act of aggression by a soldier, paramilitary or known person humiliates, degrades and demoralises. Yet even during a transitional period when a society is moving away from past violence, the violent masculinities that dominated during conflict continue.[19] In reality, violence can intensify during this transition because where there are militarised identities, easy access to guns and the 'normalisation of conflict', the 'pervasive trauma' of lingering insecurities remain.[20] The actual subjugation and inequality of women may be hidden behind the veil of new progressive laws that are prompted by the international community, but are not fully implemented when peacebuilding processes continue without ongoing international support. Yet rarely is intimate partner violence included in post-conflict assessments of political violence, because it is not viewed as an intrinsic part of the accountability of a transitional justice process. I have spent time emphasising this ongoing violence that occurs in what is called the post-conflict period to stress that this violence needs to cease before a culture of reconciliation can develop.

Gender-relational challenges to cultures of gendered violence

In what we know as the post-conflict space, international military forces are often present in the form of peacekeepers who take on additional humanitarian work. Their presence sometimes heightens an expansion of military structures with troops evident in everyday spaces.[21] It is difficult for peacebuilding to be truly effective in a culture of ongoing gendered violence and insecurity. Thus, a 'gender-relational' feminist approach in this space is 'broader' than a gender-neutral approach in not merely equating gender with women and

---

[13]Donna Pankhurst, 'Post-War Backlash Violence against Women: What can Masculinity Explain?' in *Gendered Peace: Women's Struggles for Post-War Justice and Reconciliation*, ed. Donna Pankhurst (New York: Routledge, 2008), 293.

[14]Donna Pankhurst, 'The "Sex War" and Other Wars: Towards a Feminist Approach to Peacebuilding', *Development in Practice* 13, no. 2–3 (2003): 161.

[15]Monica McWilliams and Fionnuala Ní Aoláin, '"There is a War Going on You Know": Addressing the Complexity of Violence against Women in Conflicted and Post Conflict Societies', *Transitional Justice Review* 1, no. 2 (2013): 5.

[16]Ibid., 13.

[17]Catherine O'Rourke, *Gender Politics and Transitional Justice* (London: Routledge, 2013), 38.

[18]McWilliams and Ní Aoláin, 'There is a War Going on You Know', 9.

[19]Fionnuala Ní Aoláin, 'Political Violence and Gender During Times of Transition', *Columbia Journal of Gender and Law* 15, no. 3 (2006): 830.

[20]Nahla Valji, 'Gender Justice and Reconciliation', in *Building a Future on Peace and Justice: Studies on Transitional Justice, Peace and Development*, ed. Kai Ambos et al., (Berlin: Springer-Verlag, 2009), 225.

[21]See Olivera Simić, *Regulation of Sexual Conduct in UN Peacekeeping Operations* (Dordrecht: Springer, 2012) for an analysis of differences between exploitative and non-exploitative sexual conduct of peacekeepers, and one that stresses bodily integrity, liberty and women's agency.

girls, but also with men and boys, and it is 'deeper' in examining 'the interplay between gender and other identity markers' like age, class, disability, ethnicity, religion, sexuality or urban/rural location.[22] Such a feminist approach engages holistically with the complexities of gender identities, so is more likely to further gender equality and justice. This approach is saying more than merely gender is important. It is saying that who we are is defined partly through our relationships with others, and gender plays a major role in the construction of self-identity and everyday experiences. A gender-relational approach is one that male and female peacebuilders can adopt, but it is more likely to be adopted by women who identify with the transformative potential within a feminist praxis. By feminist praxis, I mean the specific engagement of feminists whose peacebuilding and reconciliation activities embody their commitment to feminist principles and practices of gender equality and justice.

It is useful to examine one example of challenging the normality of violence. Saferworld, a UK NGO, examined the role of masculinities in driving conflict and also in building peace.[23] Their review shows how socially constructed notions of masculinity goad insecurity. The review provides examples from South Sudan and Somalia where militarised views of masculinity validate violence and motivate men and pressure women to support this violence, and from Uganda, where violence is a sign of manhood, increasing access to wealth and women. The report maintains that applying a gender perspective often assumes the need to address women's and girl's security needs, but the roles boys and men can play in prevention of conflict and peacebuilding gain less attention. Saferworld reviewed strategies used in post-conflict settings to alter attitudes that accept men's inevitable violence. The only project they identified 'which explicitly aimed to address the role of masculinities in driving militarism and conflict'[24] was a Women Peacemakers Program that trained 19 men from 17 different countries on gender-sensitive non-violence and participatory facilitation. Once back in their countries, the men initiated programs on conflict transformation that were reliant on positive masculinities. Saferworld rightly conclude that gender norms which value 'non-violence, equality, respect and tolerance' may provide some resistance to militarisation, given that gender equality is a requirement for sustainable peace.[25] A conflict that ends through 'winning' and one that ends because of respectful resolution shape habits that affect the nature of a culture of peace, I maintain, and set the scene in which reconciliation might occur.[26] A feminist gender-relational approach shows the extent to which the social acceptance of the normality of violence needs to change as a precondition to enhancing women's equality as part of peacebuilding processes.

This first section has highlighted two main shortcomings with the uncritical use of post-conflict, namely its fuzziness given remaining insecurities and the lingering culture of violence. Galtung's celebrated use of 'negative peace'[27] as the absence of widespread violent

---

[22]Henri Myrttinen, Jana Naujoks and Judy El-Bushra, *Re-Thinking Gender in Peacebuilding* (London: International Alert, 2014), 5. The authors suggest that the three main forms of peacebuilding are the following: gender-blind; focused on the women, peace and security agenda; or gender-relational.

[23]Hannah Wright, *Masculinities, Conflict and Peacebuilding: Perspectives on Men Through a Gender Lens* (London: Saferworld, 2014).

[24]Ibid., 31.

[25]Ibid., 32.

[26]Greenberg and Zuckerman, 'The Gender Dimension of Post-conflict Reconstruction'.

[27]Johann Galtung, 'Twenty-five Years of Peace Research: Ten Challenges and Responses', *Journal of Research Research* 22, no. 2 (1985): 141–58.

conflict is pertinent, because on these terms, a 'peaceful' society could ignore subtle forms of violence against women or the structural violence of gender inequality.[28] Emphases solely on direct physical violence omit the broader conceptualisations of human insecurity in everyday lives. Feminists continue to signal ways in which the post-conflict period is marked by insecurity, violence and a cultural normality of militarisation.[29] The building of 'positive peace' seeks to remove root causes of conflict, including gender inequality and gender-based violence. However, positive peace is rarely achieved fully, partially because broader ideals of economic and social justice, including gender justice are pushed aside with the urgency of stopping outbreaks of recurring violence. Peacebuilding, in having long-term goals, must attend to personal security and gender equality in order to break through the barriers of gender-blind notions of the post-conflict stage. Further, what is very relevant to a feminist gender-relational approach is that parties to reconciliation should be approximate equals.[30]

Feminists building peace and reconciliation

In this section, different ideas on what is possible in reconciliation are offered. Before doing so, I build on the former section to outline how women might comprehend how to build peace and reconciliation in ways that are consistent with feminist principles.

A transformative context for women's agency

Feminist peace and reconciliation scholars and practitioners remain committed to grasping the potential inherent in 'a post-war moment' as a prime opportunity to radically reconstruct gender relations.[31] Certainly, the integration of United Nations Security Council Resolution 1325 on women, peace and security (UNSCR 1325) into peace and security projects is now standard practice, including gender-inclusive approaches to DDR, training for peacekeepers, police and security forces and increasing the participation of women in all peace and security matters. In particular, UNSCR 1325 shifts 'the focus from "women as victims" of conflict to women as agents of transition'.[32] A feminist gender-relational approach to peacebuilding as outlined above can expedite transformational change, with case studies highlighting the role played by 'inclusivity, dialogue and empowerment'.[33] Building afresh after conflict presents openings to focus decisively on pre-conflict gender inequalities that require changed laws.[34] Transitions allow opportunities for communities to decide if cultural practices, laws and policies are outmoded, worthy of preservation or should be transformed for gender equality

---

[28]Donna Pankhurst, 'The "Sex War" and Other Wars': 156.

[29]See Cynthia Enloe, *Nimo's War, Emma's War: Making Feminist Sense of the Iraq War* (Berkley, CA: University of California Press, 2010) and Lois Handrahan, 'Conflict, Gender, Ethnicity and Post-conflict Reconstruction', *Security Dialogue* 35, no. 4 (2004): 429–45.

[30]See Louise du Toit, 'Feminism and the Ethics of Reconciliation', in *Law and the Politics of Reconciliation*, ed. Scott Veitch (Aldershot: Ashgate, 2007).

[31]Mary Moran, 'Gender, Militarism, and Peacebuilding: Projects of the Postconflict Moment', *Annual Review of Anthropology* 39 (2010): 266.

[32]Niamh Reilly, 'Seeking Gender Justice in Post-conflict Transitions: Towards a Transformative Women's Human Rights Approach', *International Journal of Law in Context* 3, no. 2 (2007): 156.

[33]Myrttinen, Naujoks and El-Bushra, 'Rethinking Gender in Peacebuilding', 6.

[34]See note 26 above.

to eventuate.[35] This does not presume the decisions will go in favour of equality; it is simply to acknowledge that a space is opened for negotiation.

It has been noted how women typically use everyday experiences to define their security needs rather than state-centric or nationalist concerns. The everyday is all-encompassing of the private, social and public realms wherein transformation is needed in order to empower women to participate as active agents.[36] Feminists highlight potential areas for such transformation in the transitional justice terrain, including accountability for past abuses, protection in the present, development of new laws, equality measures, redress, reintegration of former combatants, improving socio-economic conditions, fostering democratic governance structures and changing the cultural morés on violence, inclusivity and gender justice. Yet the 'decisions about what is included in, or left out' of transformative change processes typically are made during peace negotiations.[37] Given the paucity of women signatories to peace agreements[38], these processes rarely transform life for women.

Feminist peacebuilding praxis is broad, encompassing comprehensive, practical expectations of justice, equality, women's rights and full opportunities to practice agency. Both transitional justice and peacebuilding are intrinsically linked with practices aimed at overcoming the destructive legacies of the past to work towards a future where reconciliation is possible.[39] Transition signals a movement from one stage to another. In this movement, transformation requires 'long-term, sustainable processes' entailing economic, legal, political and psychosocial changes.[40] Intrinsic to this transformation is the need for building and sometimes rebuilding relationships between former antagonists, opponents and enemies.[41] Building non-dominating, equal relationships is intrinsic to feminist peacebuilding and is foundational to reconciliation. I seek now to explain how certain ideas written by men and women can be utilised as part of a feminist praxis for transforming relationships in building not only peace, but reconciliation also.

Different understandings of reconciliation

The meaning of the term reconciliation is, like common uses of post-conflict, often vague, used loosely or conceptually unclear. Thus, I show how reconciliation can be understood in four succinct ways that admittedly do overlap as a spectrum of possibilities, reconciling fractured relationships, a process that requires different strategies to ease relational tensions and a culture lived out in everyday practices.[42] While there is nothing intrinsically feminist

---

[35]McWilliams and Ní Aoláin, 'There is a War Going on You Know', 42.

[36]See Elisabeth Porter, 'Rethinking Women's Empowerment', *Journal of Peacebuilding & Development* 8, no. 1 (2013): 1–14.

[37]Dina Francesca Haynes, Naomi Cahn and Fionnuala Ní Aoláin, 'Women in the Post-conflict Process: Reviewing the Impact of Recent UN Actions in Achieving Gender Centrality', *Santa Clara Journal of International Law* 11 (2012): 220.

[38]A study commissioned by UNIFEM (now UN Women) showed ad hoc participation of women in track 1 peace processes, averaging 8 per cent with fewer than 3 per cent of signatories in 24 peace processes being women. See UNIFEM, 'Women's Participation in Peace Negotiations: Connections Between Presence and Influence' (New York: UNIFEM, 2010).

[39]Sarah Maddison and Laura J. Shepherd, 'Peacebuilding and the Postcolonial Politics of Transitional Justice', *Peacebuilding* 2, no. 3 (2014): 253. Their categorisation of transitional justice as thin justice, thick justice, thick transition but thin justice and thick transition with thick justice is useful.

[40]Ibid., 30.

[41]See Wendy Lambourne, 'Post-conflict Peacebuilding: Meeting Human Needs for Justice and Reconciliation', *Peace, Conflict and Development* 4 (2004): 1–24.

[42]For a full outline of these four approaches, see Elisabeth Porter, *Connecting Peace, Justice, and Reconciliation* (Boulder, CO: Lynne Rienner, 2015).

about these categorisations, they further an understanding of the limitations and possibilities for reconciliation. Later, I draw out what it means for feminists to build reconciliation as part of peacebuilding in this fourfold way.[43]

Degrees of reconciliation

First, there is a spectrum of possibilities on reconciliation. To explain the spectrum, a parallel might be made with women's groups seeking a minimum condition of equality through to feminist demanding its full realisation. For example, in writing on reconciliation, Trudy Govier writes of 'a spectrum of possibilities' from rich 'thickness' of unity to 'thinness' where there may be some willingness to engage with others, but no changed attitudes.[44] This view corresponds with Norman Porter's ideas of 'strong' and 'weak' reconciliation, where 'strong reconciliation' requires transformative changed evidenced by 'fair interactions', a space of 'common ground' and a sense of 'belonging'.[45] David Crocker contrasts 'simple coexistence' with former enemies who obey the law instead of killing each other, with a 'liberal social solidarity' where former enemies respect each other, to a 'democratic reciprocity' that 'implies a willingness to hear each other out' and even to establish just concessions that all can accept.[46]

Rajeev Bhargava writes of 'reconciliation as resignation' where people live together despite past hostility in contrast to a stronger sense of reconciliation where relationships are congenial.[47] However, Ernesto Verdeja is critical of both 'minimalist' and 'maximalist' approaches because he views a minimalist approach to be 'simple coexistence' where dealing with the past is blocked out and a maximalist approach wrongly assumes remorse.[48] Paul James' idea of 'slow reconciliation' resonates, it is where meaningful moments suggest the possibility of reconciliation, and where 'positive reconciliation' involves a continuing process of 'bringing together of persons, practices, and meanings in ongoing "places of meeting".[49] There are numerous examples of how women excel in creating these places where reconciliation can grow.[50] I am encouraging feminists to draw out this connection between building peace and fostering degrees of reconciliation.

Reconciling fractured relationships

Second, along the spectrum of possibilities, reconciliation is most commonly understood as reconciling fractured relationships. In this sense, it can be understood on a micro-level

---

[43]Jennifer J. Llewellyn and Daniel Philpott also argue that restorative justice and reconciliation are 'Partner Principles that Provide Twin Frameworks for Peacebuilding', in 'Restorative Justice and Twin Frameworks for Peacebuilding', in *Restorative Justice, Reconciliation, and Peacebuilding*, ed. Jennifer J. Llewellyn and Daniel Philpott (New York: Oxford University Press, 2014), 16.

[44]Trudy Govier, *Taking Wrongs Seriously: Acknowledgement, Reconciliation, and the Politics of Sustainable Peace* (New York: Humanity Books, 2006), 13.

[45]Porter, Norman, *The Elusive Quest: Reconciliation in Northern Ireland* (Belfast: Blackstaff Press, 2003), 94–5.

[46]David A. Crocker, 'Reckoning with Past Wrongs: A Normative Framework', in *Dilemmas of Reconciliation: Cases and Concepts*, ed. Carol A. L. Prager and Trudy Govier (Waterloo: Wilfred Laurier University Press, 2003), 54.

[47]Rajeev Bhargava, 'The Difficulty of Reconciliation', *Philosophy and Social Criticism* 38, no. 4–5 (2012): 371.

[48]Ernesto Verdeja, *Unchopping a Tree: Reconciliation in the Aftermath of Political Violence* (Philadelphia, PA: Temple University Press, 2009), 12.

[49]Paul James, 'Reconciliation: From the Usually Unspoken to the Almost Unimaginable', in *Pathways to Reconciliation: Between Theory and Practice*, ed. Philipa Rothfield, Cleo Fleming and Paul A. Komesaroff (Aldershot: Ashgate, 2008), 115, 117.

[50]See Zilka Spahić Šiljak, *Shining Humanity: Life Stories of Women Peacebuilders in Bosnia and Herzegovina* (Newcastle upon Tyne: Cambridge Scholars Publishing, 2014) for testimonies of resilience, courage and humanity in building peace and reconciliation.

to reconcile not only conflict parties, but also women and men, or between different ethnic groups of women or men of different religious beliefs. The parallels with feminist practice are clear. Building non-domineering relationships of equality is intrinsic to all branches of feminism. However, the reconciliation required in peacebuilding is between former enemies, adversaries or violent opponents who have not only felt deep anger, animosity, bitterness and resentment towards others, but they have acted on these emotions in behaviours that are cruel, murderous, shocking or wounding. Some have given orders to commit brutal acts; others have themselves committed such acts. It is important to be realistic about the enormity of developing reconciliation given the nature of the relationships under discussion. Significant groundwork in acknowledging wrongdoing and in building trust is needed for reconciliation to be contemplated.

Reconciliation, when it does happen, signals a new stage of relations or at times a fresh beginning. For many, it is the first time an amiable relationship is considered. There usually is some initial momentous 'encounter' that influences the decision to put aside previous hostilities.[51] Often, an encounter occurs when stories and acknowledgement of suffering are mutually disclosed or the first time people share a meal.[52] This acknowledgement is important because opposing sides suffer in different and sometimes similar ways. 'Acknowledgement is articulated or embodied awareness'[53] that harmful acts were committed, hurt was experienced and relationships disrupted or destroyed. On such terms, the possibilities of reconciliation can appear remote because reconciliation requires the building of trust between groups divided previously due to extreme mistrust.[54]

Just as there are degrees of reconciliation, there are degrees of trust. 'Who reconciles with whom?'[55] This is a pertinent question for women recovering from sexual violence who understandably might never want to reconcile with the perpetrator of their abuse. There should be reasonable hesitancy in too quickly equating forgiveness with reconciliation. In the absence of acknowledgement of wrongdoing, demonstration of genuine remorse and apology, forgiveness is certainly a gift, but it is not one all victims are ready to give. For many victims of sexual abuse, reconciliation with perpetrators of abuse cannot be contemplated, nor is it desirable if there is any danger of psychological harm continuing.

While certain men stress a progressive, 'negotiated view of reconciliation as forging new social relations',[56] reconciling fractured relationships undoubtedly is a feminist practice in situations where people are willing to break down destructive patterns of domination and inequality. This view of reconciliation could be stressed more explicitly by feminists, not to claim any exclusivity of the practice, but to build further on the rich body of feminist

---

[51]John Paul Lederach, *Building Peace. Sustainable Reconciliation in Divided Societies* (Washington, DC: UN Institute of Peace, 2004), 26.

[52]Susan McKay shows how for women acknowledgement of gender injustice extends beyond rape and sexual torture to multiple examples of domestic slavery, disappearance of family members, poverty, forced prostitution because of food shortage or poor security, in 'Gender Justice and Reconciliation', *Women's Studies International Forum* 23, no. 5 (2000): 564. Many women's grass roots peacebuilding groups link gender justice with reconciliation processes. However, as McKay argues: 'There is no substantive discussion of gender and reconciliation in … reconciliation literature', 566–7. This is the key issue this article is addressing.

[53]Trudy Govier, 'A Dialectic of Acknowledgement', in *Reconciliation(s): Transitional Justice in Postconflict Societies*, ed. Joanna R. Quinn (Montreal: McGill-Queen's University Press, 2009), 41.

[54]Ibid., 49.

[55]Toshihoro Abe, 'Reconciliation as Process or Catalyst: Understanding the Concept in a Post-conflict Society', *Comparative Sociology* 11 (2012): 787.

[56]Phil Clark, 'Negotiating Reconciliation in Rwanda: Popular Challenges to the Official Discourse of Post-Genocide National Unity', *Journal of Intervention and Statebuilding* (2014): 7.

scholarship on empathetic relationships. As feminists highlight, a relational understanding of selves stresses the connections we have with others.[57] The nature of relationships affects significantly our notions of who we are in our social and communal lives. 'Human lives are led narratively' and war disrupts individual, communal and national narratives.[58] Reconciliation is important because it can allow parties to deal with the harms to relationships caused by these violent disruptions.

Interpersonal exchanges required by reconciliation processes highlight 'the non-linear, constantly negotiated "everyday" dynamics that determine whether or not parties believe they have reconciled' and, in Rwanda for example, they include direct interactions like sitting together at church, eating and drinking together, caring for each other's children and working on each other's farms.[59] For women, these everyday dynamics often involve battling to cope with the inequality of disrespectful gendered relationships and all the emotions that accompany feeling devalued. They also involve living beside men who have abused their bodies. Appreciating such dynamics should heighten understanding of the reasonable reluctance to reconcile when the harm caused through acts like sexual violence destroy self-dignity. Reconciliation of relationships should never be forced.

Reconciliation processes

Third, in addition to being a spectrum of possibilities and a practice of re/building relationships, reconciliation requires appropriate processes. Violent conflict damages the social framework of communities, destroying trust, belonging and cohesion. The processes of reconciliation seek to facilitate dialogue with people for whom interaction has faltered or been non-existent, and here, it aligns closely with peacebuilding.[60] Where deep discord has complex historical roots, openness to difference must deal with the pain and fear of the unknown. Feminist politics of difference, seen particularly in a 'transversal politics' where 'identity, positioning and values' are part of the struggle between divided groups[61], broadens debates on an openness to difference between the Global South and North, but rarely translates into ideas and practices of reconciliation. In the processes of reconciliation, dialogue is crucial as vulnerable yet curious parties explore how their beliefs, emotions and narratives diverge and sometimes 'come together'.[62]

Dialogue involves opening up spaces where multiple voices can be heard. In these dialogical spaces, disagreements persist, but when there is a desire for reconciliation, the hostility of differences that were often causes of violence is minimised. These spaces 'between speaking and listening' are often risky as significant differences are aired.[63] Part of the risk lies in accepting the responsibility for the relational harm done. Giving voice to the silenced

---

[57]See for example Christine Koggel, *Perspectives on Equality Constructing a Relational Theory* (Lanham, MD: Rowman and Littlefield, 1998) and Catriona Mackenzie and Natalie Stoljar, eds., *Relational Autonomy: Feminist Perspectives on Autonomy, Agency, and the Social Self* (Oxford: Oxford University Press, 2000).

[58]Susan Dwyer, 'Reconciliation for Realists', in *Dilemmas of Reconciliation: Cases and Concepts*, ed. Carol A. L. Prager and Trudy Govier (Waterloo: Wilfrid Laurier University Press, 2003), 96, 100.

[59]Clark, 'Negotiating Reconciliation in Rwanda' 9: 14.

[60]Elizabeth Cole, 'Reconciliation as a Peacebuilding Practice: New Questions, New Ideas', *USIP Insights* Fall (2014): 2.

[61]See Cynthia Cockburn, *The Line: Women, Partition and the Gender Order in Cyprus* (London: Zed Books, 2004), 172 and Nira Yuval-Davis, *The Politics of Belonging: Intersectional Contestations* (London: Sage, 2011).

[62]Barbara S. Tint, 'Dialogue, Forgiveness, and Reconciliation', in *Forgiveness and Reconciliation: Psychological Pathways to Conflict Transformation and Peace Building*, eds. Ani Kalayjian and Raymond F. Paloutzian (Dordrecht: Springer, 2010), 271.

[63]Elisabeth Porter, 'Risks and Responsibilities: Creating Dialogical Spaces in Northern Ireland', *International Feminist Journal of Politics* 2, no. 2 (2000): 178.

through this type of deliberative enquiry is fundamental to feminism.[64] Many men obviously are experienced in such enquiry, but there is ample anecdotal and empirical evidence that women peacebuilders excel in giving voice to the silenced and in working across coalitions of ethno-religious differences in order to build the trust which is a necessary part of the process of reconciliation.[65] Through dialogue, there is a humanisation of the other, in moving away from a fractured, antagonistic past to new possibilities of reconciled relations.

Culture of reconciliation

Fourth, the relationship-building and the processes of reconciliation occur in a culture of reconciliation that stands as a visible contrast to the militarised violence explained in the first section of this article. Changing the culture of masculinised, oppositional workplaces, organisations, relationships and societies is fundamental to feminism. Changing cultural attitudes and practices that normalise violence is also an imperative in peacebuilding and is necessary for reconciliation to thrive.

In order for a new culture of gender equality, inclusive human rights and mutual respect to prevail, significant changes of attitudes are needed. A culture of reconciliation 'must be embodied', it cannot merely be confined to the symbolic realm, it must be lived out in new practices and relationships at all levels.[66] In addition to normative reasons why reconciliation is a good thing in restoring once antagonistic relationships or in building newly created ones, there are sound reasons for building a culture of reconciliation where decent relationships exist. Former adversaries need to live close to each other, work together and share social spaces.

An example highlights this point. Sadako Ogata, former UN High Commissioner for Refugees, writing of her experience of those returning to Bosnia, reflects on her exposure to hatred.[67] The commission was preparing roofs, doors and windows of shelters for returnees. She tells the story of a Serbian woman who had gone back to a Bosnian-dominated community. The woman told Ogata that on her return, the house was intact, but 'none of her former neighbours would talk to her'.[68] This tense culture is the reality in which the 'relational reconstruction'[69] of reconciliation occurs. The point that many women grasp this relationality in a profound sense should not be overstated because essentialist accounts of peaceful femininity are readily discredited by the numbers of female combatants or the negative socialisation of mothers who encourage sons to be warriors, or who perpetuate an othering of difference in their interactions with others.

Nevertheless, I argue that many women are immersed in nurturing cultures of relationships. Further, a gender balance in peace processes can alter the aggressive milieu in which antagonisms are worked through, creating a positive culture where victim harms are prioritised and processes of reconciliation are more likely to emerge. Reconciling what it means

---

[64]See for example, Brooke Ackerly, *Political Theory and Feminist Social Criticism* (Cambridge: Cambridge University Press, 2000).

[65]See Sanam Naraghi Anderlini, *Women Building Peace. What They Do, Why it Matters* (Boulder, CO: Lynne Rienner, 2007).

[66]Andrew Rigby, *Justice and Reconciliation: After the Violence* (Boulder, CO: Lynne Rienner, 2001), 189.

[67]In Antonio Chayes and Martha Minow, eds., *Imagine Coexistence: Restoring Humanity after Violent Ethnic Conflict* (San Francisco, CA: Jossey-Bass, 2003), xiv.

[68]Ibid.

[69]Graeme Simpson, 'Reconciliation Beyond Conceptual Debates', *USIP Insights* Fall (2014): 7.

to live in peace, rather than in war, needs changes of mindset, practices, expectations and cultural norms. There are extensive cultural differences in understandings of reconciliation[70] and in building cultures of reconciliation through indigenous practices, cleansing rituals, dramatisation, customary trauma healing and restorative justice.[71]

I find it remarkable how few contributions to this overview of four different ways to conceptualise reconciliation are written by women or from a feminist perspective. This matters for two reasons. First, a consideration of the lingering violence of the post-war period where reconciliation occurs is needed and feminists are well-suited to reminding peacebuilders of this. Second, feminist have highlighted women's relational skills[72] in international relations and security studies, but rarely link peacebuilding and reconciliation. This link warrants more attention.

Beyond post-conflict

In this third section, I make the case further for why feminists should contribute more explicitly to the reconciliation space. Feminists agree on the need to understand the gendered nature of the post-conflict context, primarily to make a case for what is needed to respond effectively to gender-specific needs. Where there is a less explicit feminist voice is on the value of reconciliation. Speculation on why this is the case is not straightforward. Unless there is an engendering of transitional justice, any reconciliation that does occur may be based on 'pre-conflict inequitable power relations' and thus can only be partial, thereby subverting the transformative potential to make key changes to gender justice.[73] Once the need for gender centrality of a feminist-relational approach is acknowledged and implemented in transitional contexts, I argue that there are good reasons for feminists to further scholarship on and practices of reconciliation. Most feminist work on reconciliation to date relates to truth commissions and empathy. On these issues, feminists highlight attention to the voices of victims and the restorative justice principles implicit in most commissions overlap with feminist ones in affirming the moral worth of all involved, including victims, remorseful perpetrators and local aggrieved communities.

For example, the South African Truth and Reconciliation Commission (TRC) was based on the premise that reconciliation is required as part of 'building a non-racial and *non-sexist* democracy'.[74] A feminist perspective gives voice to the needs of powerless women victims. Commission reports from Haiti, Liberia, Morocco, Peru, Sierra Leone, South Africa and Timor-Leste include sections 'on gender-specific crimes or on the experience of women in the conflict'.[75] These are important in redressing gender-blind analyses, but rarely are they specific on feminist consequences for reconciliation. Some readers might suggest that this lack does not matter. I think it does in selling women and men, and women in particular,

---

[70]See Joanna Quinn's research where Ugandans gave wide ranging responses to what they understood as reconciliation, in Joanna Quinn ed., *Reconciliation(s): Transitional Justice in Postconflict Societies* (Montreal: McGill-Queens University Press, 2009), 183.

[71]See Jens Meierhenrich, 'Varieties of Reconciliation', *Law and Social Enquiry* 33, no. 1 (2008): 195–231.

[72]I do not imply any feminine pacifist essentialism, but refer to women's prime nurturing responsibilities, willingness to develop coalitions across major differences and their proclivity to empathetic listening.

[73]Valji, 'Gender Justice and Reconciliation', 235.

[74]Rina Kashyap, 'Exploring the Narrative of Truth: A Feminist Critique of the South African Truth and Reconciliation Commission' (paper presented at ISA's 49th annual convention, 'Bridging Multiple Divides', San Francisco, CA, USA, March 26, 2008), 4.

[75]Priscilla B. Hayner, *Unspeakable Truths: Transitional Justice and the Challenge of Truth Commissions*. 2nd ed. New York: Routledge, 2011, 89.

short, in what a feminist approach potentially offers, particularly in supporting empathetic practices. It is necessary to keep qualifying, some men demonstrate empathy in their peacebuilding and reconciliation work, and some women are harsh, intolerant and refuse to recognise the validity of others' viewpoints and empathy is not conspicuous in their everyday lives. However, it is feminist scholarship and praxis that lead the way in linking empathy, compassion and deconstructing the antagonism towards the other,[76] and I assert that more feminist work is needed to extend these links to reconciliation. In exploring empathy and truth-telling, the aim is to envision further how feminists building peace and reconciliation might do so in ways that go beyond the narrow confines of gender-blind concepts of the post-conflict.

Empathy

Sympathy is demonstrated through a sharing of emotions such as grief or pain. With empathy, one tries to imagine what it would be like to, for example, lose one's relatives through genocide or have a daughter raped in war by a neighbour. Barriers to demonstrating empathy post-war are massive for men and women, including feelings of betrayal, discrimination, fear, ethno-religious group pressures, mistrust, stereotypes and recurring violence. Empathy does not require agreement or negation of differences, because the workable relationships that result because of reconciliation abound in differences in trying to comprehend the world from the perspective of another.

Active, empathetic listening in safe spaces is not exclusive to women, but it is fundamental to feminist praxis. When reconciliation is the desired outcome rather than mere coexistence, 'an empathic connection must occur'.[77] This connection permits a reconciliation that challenges dehumanisation and deliberately sets out to rehumanise the 'other' through an empathetic imagining and understanding of the perspective of another person.[78] This identification with someone is necessary to 'inspire the agency needed to successfully embrace reconciliation'.[79] Often there remains uneasiness with some of these differences; nevertheless, in meaningful reconciliation, there is a respect for differences. Here, connections between peacebuilding and reconciliation are obvious. Without the conditions created by individuals, NGOs and practitioners building peace, the conditions to create trust, voice disagreement civilly and find ways to relate meaningfully despite significant differences, reconciliation cannot occur, in anything other than occasional individual interactions. In a truth and reconciliation commission, empathy typically occurs through humanising interactions because 'forgiveness and reconciliation requires courage, commitment, and compassion'.[80]

---

[76]See Fiona Robinson, *Globalising Care. Ethics, Feminist Theory, and International Relations* (Boulder, CO: Westview Press, 1999) and Selma Sevenhuijsen, *Citizenship and the Ethics of Care. Feminist Considerations on Justice, Morality and Politics* (London: Routledge, 1998).

[77]Jodi Halpern and Harvey M. Weinstein, 'Rehumanizing the Other: Empathy and Reconciliation', *Human Rights Quarterly* 26, no. 3 (2004): 567.

[78]Ibid., 568.

[79]Emma Hutchison and Roland Bleiker, 'Emotional Reconciliation: Reconstituting Identity and Community after Trauma', *European Journal of Social Theory* 11, no. 3 (2008): 395.

[80]Paula Green, 'Reconciliation and Forgiveness in Divided Societies: A Path of Courage, Compassion, and Commitment', in *Forgiveness and Reconciliation: Psychological Pathways to Conflict Transformation and Peace Building*, ed. Ani Kalayjian and Raymond F. Paloutzian (Dordrecht: Springer, 2010), 255.

Truth and reconciliatory spaces

In moving beyond limited gender-neutral notions of post-conflict, it is clear that reconciliatory spaces occur in multiple settings such as around the negotiating table, in tribunals, commissions and new corridors of power. However, there is ample evidence that these spaces remain dominated by men.[81] Frequently, the meaning-making of complex narratives of women arises in informal settings where people relax and feel secure. These settings might be around a kitchen table, under a tree, in a playground, on the grass or on a mat in a hut. Sometimes they transpire through the use of theatre, drama, art, play or healing workshops, wherever people are open to express their individual stories and learn about others.

This form of open storytelling has proven to be very useful in women's groups. For example, *Duhozanye* ('To Console Each Other') is a group of Hutu and Tutsi women who came together in mourning, having lost family members, most had been raped and many had borne children through this violation.[82] The relational bonds that developed in the group led to building houses and starting an agricultural cooperative, a school for orphaned children and a craft centre. Through collective mourning, these women developed a common narrative that provides a safe place for practical manifestations of reconciliation between Hutu and Tutsi women as an indigenous, bottom-up 'narrative transformation'.[83] Feelings of mutual empathetic legitimation are important to a meaningful reconciliation. To feminists, mutuality confirms equality of respect.

Knowing how to respond to the telling of a story about harms suffered in conflict involves intense sensitivity. The hope is that through telling one's story and in being listened to, damaged survivors can reclaim their identities. In witnessing to narratives that deal with the traumatic past, typically in truth commissions where perpetrators of abuse are present and feel remorse, 'victims find their voice to speak the unspeakable', and perpetrators 'confront the consequences of their actions' in a public context.[84] In this 'witnessing dance', victim and perpetrator speak to each other and bear witness to the stories they bring. Through doing so, perpetrators of abuse rehumanise the victim–survivor and both can reclaim their own sense of humanity. This is only possible when the perpetrator is remorseful and the victim is willing to confront the perpetrator. Even then, the degree of reconciliation might be minimal.

The special hearings of women's experiences in the South African TRC bear witness to the idea that the 'telling of pain is an act of intimacy'.[85] In giving testimonies, individual incidents of violence were converted from narratives of pain into stories of human rights violations. Witnessing to such testimonies recognises and acknowledges suffering through attentive listening to highly emotive accounts 'of memory, loss, and grief'.[86] Such accounts express pain through words, gestures and sometimes through intentional silence. Women's deliberate silence is a meaningful act of agency, recognised only through probing 'the cadences of silences, the gaps between the fragile words, in order to hear what it is that

---

[81]O'Rourke, *Gender Politics and Transitional Justice.*

[82]Sara Cobb, *Speaking of Violence: The Politics and Poetics of Narrative Dynamics in Conflict Resolution* (Oxford: Oxford University Press, 2013).

[83]Ibid., 103.

[84]Pumla Gobodo-Madikezela, 'Trauma, Forgiveness and the Witnessing Dance: Making Public Spaces Intimate', *Journal of Analytical Psychology* 53 (2008): 176.

[85]Fiona Ross, *Bearing Witness: Women and the Truth and Reconciliation Commission in South Africa* (London: Pluto Press, 2003), 6.

[86]Ibid., 15.

women say'.[87] Yet expressing one's suffering or deliberately keeping quiet about it does not necessarily lead to the healed subject.

Given the need for a gender perspective on stories told in truth commissions, the question needs to be asked 'of how, by whom, against whom, and in what context this sexual violence is taking place?'[88] In the South African TRC, differential gender repercussions of narratives of harm were mistakenly identified as the reluctance of women to testify of the direct harm they suffered 'as silence caused by reticence, proprietary, or lack of education about rights'.[89] This was not the case, because for many, silence was self-chosen agency. Silence enabled women to protect their dignity and for those in public positions, their reputation also. Such findings are a reminder that the presence of gender experts in truth-telling contexts is essential in order to understand the gender-sensitive requirements of responding to deep suffering. Narratives of violence call for 'trust in the capacity to attend to suffering'.[90] An empathic engagement with the unspoken silences[91] and the spoken words of pain, links attentiveness with the responsibility to respond, which I argue is the hallmark of feminist articulations of compassion.[92] Compassion is exhibited in appropriate responses to harms.

To summarise, telling the truth succeeds where the narrator's story is acknowledged and dignity is restored. Listening requires patience to hear what is said. Listening is 'the attending to a sharp sense of what things mean'.[93] Listening to the story of a victim is one thing, what about empathy to someone responsible for inflicting suffering? When perpetrators express feelings of remorse, it can present them as the 'wounded other',[94] showing concern towards the harmed other, feeling troubled by their evil actions and the damage they have caused. An empathic change towards the other can begin a reconciliatory relationship. This change should not be overstated. Most perpetrators of abuse do not change. When they do, compassion is an important response to the person who is suffering. Through compassionate responses, particular needs can be met and dignity is restored. Such compassion unites justice and care and can lead to reconciliation.

Conclusion

Reconciliatory spaces are multiple. Within these spaces, men and women need to feel free to argue and disagree; they also need opportunities to apologise, confess, forgive, build trust and develop changed relationships that show the healing power of reconciliation. A feminist peacebuilding and reconciliation lens illuminates these spaces. In doing so, I have made three main arguments.

First, I have demonstrated that feminist constructions of peace and reconciliation are needed, ones that are aware of the complexities of the so-called post-conflict period where a culture of violence remains, particularly for women whose partners were combatants and

---

[87]Ibid., 50.

[88]Hayner, *Unspeakable Truths*, 88.

[89]Fiona Ross, 'An Acknowledged Failure: Women, Voice, Violence, and the South African Truth and Reconciliation Commission', in *Localizing Transitional Justice: Interventions and Priorities after Mass Violence*, ed. Rosalind Shaw and Lars Waldorf (Stanford, CA: Stanford University Press, 2010), 74–5.

[90]Ibid., 79.

[91]See Elisabeth Porter, 'Gendered Narratives: Stories and Silences in Transitional Justice', *Human Rights Review* (2016).

[92]See Elisabeth Porter, 'Can Politics Practice Compassion?' *Hypatia: A Journal of Feminist Philosophy* 21, no. 4 (2006): 97–123.

[93]John Paul Lederach, *The Moral Imagination: The Art and Soul of Building Peace* (Oxford: Oxford University Press, 2005), 70.

[94]Gobodo-Madikizela, 'Trauma, Forgiveness and the Witnessing Dance', 344.

in places where a militarised security presence remains. The term post-war captures this period more accurately. I argued that the transition from conflict towards sustainable peace provides opportunities for transformed relationships. Such transformation lies at the heart of peacebuilding and reconciliation and also is fundamental to feminist practice.

Second, I explained a four-fold approach to understanding diverse views on reconciliation. Even though these understandings are not written from a feminist perspective, they provide indication of how feminists might become more engaged with the literature and the ensuing practices. Such engagement might also assist women at local, community, NGO and political levels to work through the difficult but rewarding stages of trust-building and open dialogue, both necessary to move towards reconciliation.

Third, I used empathy and truth-telling as examples of feminist engagement with reconciliation. Feminist practitioners and scholars emphasise empathetic listening to victims' accounts of suffering, and without a compassionate response, the telling of stories do not necessarily lead to healing. The concrete response is the practical outcome of compassion. I suggest that there are additional avenues that feminists could pursue to integrate peacebuilding with reconciliation. These may include international NGOs working with local women's organisations, programs in education directed towards understanding the benefits of reconciliation, attention to reconciliation as a consequence of memory work in museums and across the full gamut of peacebuilding work. Meaningful reconciliation can never be forced. In explaining how feminists can work within multiple spaces of reconciliation across a spectrum of possibilities, in re/building relationships, developing processes and fostering peaceful cultures, the discourse of peacebuilding and reconciliation can begin the long path of moving beyond narrow post-conflict frameworks.

Disclosure statement

No potential conflict of interest was reported by the author.

Index

Abukakar, Bai Cabaybay 28
access to exclusive processes 18, 25–7
advocacy for women in peace 18–20, 23, 27–8
Afghanistan 6
Africa 73–88
'Africa Rising' 78–9
African nowhere 78–80
African Union 24, 27, 74, 78–9
Afrocentric agency 81
agency analysis 39–40
Agenda 2063 79
agents of change 3–5, 7–8, 94–5
alternative accounts of subjecthood 75–8
ambiguity 90–92
amnesia 4
anal rape 66
Anderlini, Sanam 4, 19
Angola 63
apathy 4
application of 'gender lens' to peace 1–2, 50
Arawa Peace Conference 52
Auchter, Jessica 81–2
autonomy 52

backlash of war 63, 91–2
Ban Ki-Moon 16
Bangladesh 7
Barnes, Charles 51
barriers to women 28–9
better understanding of exclusion 37–40
beyond post-conflict 89–104; conclusion 103–4;
    empathy 101–3; feminist reconciliation 94–100;
    fuzzy post-conflict periods 90–94; gendered
    nature of post-conflict context 100–101
Bhargava, Rajeev 96
binary gender logic 29–30, 41–2, 83
Björkdahl, Annika 47, 49–50
blueprint approach to peacebuilding 71–2
border thinking 73–88
Bosnia 99
Bougainville see post-conflict Bougainville
Bougainville Revolutionary Army 51–2
BRA see Bougainville Revolutionary Army
building peace and reconciliation 94–100

Burundi 22, 24–5, 28

canon of WPS 3
ceasefires 90–92
Chapultepec Peace Agreement 17
Charlesworth, Hilary 4, 20, 51
Chile 41
Cockburn, Cynthia 4, 40
Cohn, Carol 3
collectivity 42
Colombia 19
compassion 103; see also empathy
conflict and gender 50–53; women as conflict
    protagonists 51; women as peace protagonists
    51–3
conflict protagonists 51
conflict transition 47
conflict vs. post-conflict 90–92
connecting to study of sexual violence 65–8
Connell, R.W. 64
constitution of political activity 6–7
constructing peacebuilding fetish 54–6
construction of African nowhere 78–80
contributing to reconciliation space 100–101
Conzinc Rio Tinto Australia 50
Coomaraswamy, Radhika 4
Coronel-Ferrer, Miriam 28
Corrigan, Mairead 19
corruption 81
CRA see Conzinc Rio Tinto Australia
creating access to exclusive processes 25–7
critical friendship 44
critics of 'liberal peace' 71–2
Croatia 8
Crocker, David 96
culture of reconciliation 99–100
cultures of gendered violence 66, 92–4

Darfur Peace Agreement 22–5, 27
Davies, S. 68
DDR see Disarmament, Demobilisation and
    Rehabilitation
debunking generalisations 19–20
decoloniality 74–7, 83–5

INDEX

decolonising gender 73–88; African gendered nowhere 78–80; conclusion 85–7; importance of mundanity 83–5; masks and *Menschen* 80–83; unbearable coloniality 75–8
degrees of reconciliation 96
delinking 85–7
Democratic Republic of Congo 22, 24–8, 65, 82–5
Department for International Development (UK) 32
deprivation 52
DfID *see* Department for International Development (UK)
Diamond, Larry 35
different understandings of reconciliation 95–6
Disarmament, Demobilisation and Rehabilitation 10, 68–70, 82, 91
dissidence 48–9
'doing' inclusion 38
domestic violence 24, 61–2, 69
donor funding 82–3
DRC *see* Democratic Republic of Congo
Dultozanye 102

Eade, Deborah 55
'economic empowerment' 8–9
economic well-being 41, 91
El Salvador 17, 23, 28, 66–7
El-Bushra, Judy 63
embedded relationships 36–7
emergence of political settlement 33–6
empathy 101–4; truth and reconciliation spaces 102–3
'enemy' women 59–72
Enlightenment 77
Enloe, Cynthia 36
essential nature of women's participation 13–15, 29–30
essentialism 4
essentialist binary gender logic 29–30
Eurocentric assumptions 74
everyday peacebuilding 83–5
exclusion 25–7, 37–44, 47; understanding better 37–40

Farabundo Marti Front for National Liberation 17
femicide 63
Feminist of Color Collective 44
feminist curiosity 36
feminist frontiers 73–88; taming the West 85–7
feminist insight 36–40; understanding exclusion 37–40
feminist perspective on peacebuilding 31–45
feminist reconciliation 89–104
feminist vanguard 86
feminists building peace 94–100; culture of reconciliation 99–100; degrees of reconciliation 96; reconciliation processes 98–9; reconciling fractured relationships 96–8; understandings of reconciliation 95–6; women's agency 94–5
fetishisation of peace 48, 54–6

Fierke, Karin M. 84
FMLN *see Farabundo Marti Front for National Liberation*
forced migration 34
forces vives 25
Foucault, Michel 76
fractured relationships 96–8
framework for substantive representation 20–22
friction and peacebuilding 48–50, 53–7; peacebuilding fetish 54–6; shadows cast 56–7
fuzzy post-conflict periods 90–94; ambiguity between conflict and post-conflict 90–92; cultures of gendered violence 92–4

Galtung, Johann 93–4
gang warfare 67–8
Garusu, Lorraine (Sister) 53
gender blindness 32–3, 89–90, 100–101
gender dynamics of peacemaking 1–15
gender and friction 48–50
gender mainstreaming 9–13, 60–61
gender relational challenges 92–4
gender sensitivity 73–4
gender silence 79
gender-relational approaches 82, 92–4
gendered African nowhere 78–80
gendered faultlines 34–5
gendered identity 64
gendered nationalism 34
gendered peace 75–8
gendered violence cultures 92–4
gendering UN peacebuilding 5–13; 'economic empowerment' of women 8–9; gender mainstreaming 9–13; women in peacebuilding discourse 6–7; women as victims/agents of change 7–8
glass ceiling 36
global coloniality 76–9
globalisation 47
global–local discourse 47–50, 57
Goetz, Anne-Marie 36
Govier, Trudy 96
grey literature 47–8
'groundhog day' negotiations 43
Guatemala 21–6, 28, 63
Gwboee, Lemah 19

Hakena, Helen 53
Handrahan, Lori 40
healing power of reconciliation 103–4
hegemonic masculinity 64
helpless victims 5
Hermkens, Anna Karina 52
hierarchies in political settlement 40–41
his-story lessons 5–13
HIV 61
Hobbes, Thomas 85
Högland, Christina 47, 49–50
how war impacts ex-combatant males 65–70
hyper-masculinity 64; *see also* 'problem with men'

INDEX

ICD *see* Inter-Congolese Dialogue
impacts of war 68–70
importance of mundanity 83–5
including women's needs 41–4
inclusion 38, 41–4
incommeasurability 43–4
insecure post-conflict periods 90–94
Inter-Congolese Dialogue 24–5, 29
inter-elite bargaining 35–7, 39–40
inter-personal violence 71–2
International Criminal Court 61
international fraternity 40
intersectionality 37–40, 43
Islam 24–5
Israel 67

Jabri, Vivienne 75–6
Jajurie, Raissa 28
James, Paul 96
Jean-Bouchard, Évelyne 82–3
Jenkins, Robert 36
Jerven, Morten 78–9
Johnson-Sirleaf, Ellen 28

Kandiyoti, Deniz 83
Khan, Mushtaq 41

learning from his-story 5–13
Leitana Nehan Women's Development Agency 53
liberal peace 41–4, 71–2, 86
liberal–local hybridity 77
Liberia 19
light, heat, shadows 46–58
listening 102–3
LNWDA *see* Leitana Nehan Women's
    Development Agency
lobbying 25–6, 49
Lugones, Maria 76, 82–3

MacGinty, Roger 60
male ex-combatants 68–70
male survivors of war trauma 59–72
malleability of power 37
'Mama Maria' 52
Mandela, Nelson 28
marginalisation 80
Marian traditions 52
Marxism 76–7
masculinities and hierarchies 40–41
'masculinity' as explanatory factor 63–5
masks 80–83
materiality 86; *see also* mundanity
matrilineal authority 55
mediation 20, 23–4
meeting women's needs/interests 41–4
men as victims of sexual violence 65–8
Mendez, Luz 28
Menschen 80–83
mental ill health 68–70
messiahs 81–2

metageographies 78–80
methods of feminism 36–40
micro-coloniality 84
Mignolo, Walter D. 77, 84
MILF *see* Moro Islamic Liberation Front
military codes 67
Moro Islamic Liberation Front 24–6, 28–9
'Mother' Africa 87
mourning 102
Mudimbe, Valentin 78
mundanity 83–5
Murguialday, Clara 17

Nabukeera-Musoke, Harriet 29
naming masculinities 40–41
Nasioi tribe 51
Ndovlu-Gatsheni, Sabelo 79
negative peace 93–4
neoliberal shackles 74
Ngũgĩ wa Thiong'o 86
Nobel Peace Prize 19
non-compliance 64
non-hierarchical dialogue 43–4
non-sexist democracy 100–101
normalising violence 99–100
norms of honour 48
Northern Ireland 19, 41
Nyerere, Julius 28

O'Donnell, Guillermo 35
of masks and *Menschen* 80–83
Ogala, Sadako 99
Ona, Frances 51
oral rape 66

Palestine 67
Pan-Africanism 81
Panel of the Wise 79
Papua New Guinea *see* post-conflict Bougainville
patriarchy 33–4, 40, 76
peace protagonists 51–3
Peacebuilding in the Aftermath of Conflict 6
peacebuilding discourse 6–7
peacebuilding fetish 54–7; shadows cast by 56–7
peacebuilding and gender 48–50
peacebuilding and WPS agenda 13–15
peripherisation 29–30
persistent barriers to women 28–9
pervasive trauma 92
phenomenon of post-war violence 62–3
Philippines 24, 26, 28–9
Pihei, Rose 53
PNG Security Force 50–51, 57
Poland 41
political settlement analysis 31–45; conclusion
    44–5; feminist insight 36–40; including women's
    needs 41–4; masculinities/hierarchies 40–41;
    roots of political settlement 33–6
Porter, Norman 96
positive peace 94; *see also* negative peace

INDEX

post-anthropocentric future 83–4
post-conflict Bougainville 46–58; conclusion 58; gender and conflict in 50–53; gender and friction in 53–7; gender, friction, peacebuilding 48–50
post-conflict periods 90–94
post-human agency 85
post-war violence against women 62–3
postcolonialism 76–8
posttraumatic stress disorder 69
'problem with men' 59–72; 'masculinity' as explanation 63–5
processes of exclusion 25–7
processes of reconciliation 98–9
psychiatric intervention 70
PTSD *see* posttraumatic stress disorder

Quijano, Aníbal 76

racialised peace 75–8
rape 50–52, 59–72, 80–83, 102
re-politicisation of peacebuilding 75–6
reconciliation 94–100; degrees of 96; processes of 98–9; understandings of 95–6
reconciling fractured relationships 96–8
relational harm 98–9
Renaissance 77
repression 34
reproductive labour 77–8
rest of the world 85–7
revisiting violence against women 59–72; conclusion 71–2; impacts of war on ex-combatant men 68–70; 'masculinity' as a factor 63–5; post-war violence 62–3; problem for peacebuilding 60–62; study of sexual violence 65–8
Richmond, Oliver P. 60
Rooney, Ellish 38
roots of political settlement 33–6
Rwanda 63, 81, 98

Sa'ar, Amalia 83
Sabaratnam, Meera 74
sacred connections 51–2
SADC *see* Southern African Development Community
Saferworld 93
Schmitter, Philippe C. 35
Schutte, Ofelia 43–4
seats at the table 16–30
secessionist warfare 47
second wave feminism 59–60
'secondary critiques' 71–2
security sector reform 80–87
selection effect 19
self-chosen agency 103
Self–Other relations 77, 85–7
Selimovic, Anna 47
separatism 50
Serero, Perpetua 51

sex drive 66
sexual looting 67–8
sexual violence 59–72
sexualised and gender-based violence 8, 78–83, 85–6; *see also* rape; sexual violence
sexually transmitted diseases 34
SGBV *see* sexualised and gender-based violence
shadows cast by peacebuilding fetish 56–7
Sierra Leone 6, 63, 65, 100
Sirivi, Josephine 53, 55
Smart, Carol 35
soap 91
Somalia 93
South African Truth and Reconciliation Commission 100, 102–3
Southern African Development Community 80
spaces for truth 102–3
Sri Lanka 67
SSR *see* security sector reform
status quo vs. transformation 44–5
STDs *see* sexually transmitted diseases
stealth approach 8–9
stigma 34
storytelling 102–3
study of masculinities 65–8
subject of women in peacebuilding discourse 6–7
subjectivity 14, 81, 83–4
subordination 18
substantive peace 22–3
substantive representation 16–30
Sudan 22–3, 27, 29, 93
'superheroines' 4
Sustainable Development Goal 16 79
Swaine, Aisling 38
Synthesis Report 7, 10–11

taking a 'gender perspective' 9–13
taming the West 85–7
Tanzania 91
terrorism 84
transformative context 94–5
transitional justice 92, 95, 100
Transitional Justice Institute 21
trauma 59–60, 66–72, 91–2, 100–102
TRC *see* South African Truth and Reconciliation Commission
'Triple-A' syndrome 4
Tripp, Marie 6–7
True, J. 68
trust 97, 104
truth and reconciliatory spaces 102–3
Tsing, Anna 47, 49–50

Uganda 19, 22, 24–5, 28–9, 63, 93
UN Peacebuilding Commission 2, 5–6, 10–15
UN Rule of Law assistance 10
UN Women 24
unbearable coloniality 75–8
understanding exclusion better 37–40
understanding reconciliation 95–6

INDEX

understanding women's representation 16–30; advocating for women 27–8; conclusion 29–30; creating access to processes 25–7; framework for representation 20–22; persistent barriers 28–9; women with an agenda 23–5; women in peace? 18–20; women's substantive peace 22–3

Unidad Revolucionaria Nacional Guatemalteca 28

UNIFEM 24–8

Unmensch 80–82

UNSCR 1325 1–18, 20–25, 28–30, 47–9, 54, 58, 94–5

Uppsala Conflict Data Program 21

URNG *see Unidad Revolucionaria Nacional Guatemalteca*

US Army 68–9

validity of women's contribution 58

Verdeja, Ernesto 96

victims of violence? 3–5

vigilance 48

violence against women 60–62

violent post-conflict periods 90–94

vulnerability to violence 91–2

Waylen, Georgina 29

'web of harms' 92

Williams, Betty 19

'witnessing dance' 102

women with an agenda 23–5

'women of color' 82

women as conflict protagonists 51

women and peace processes 16–30

Women, Peace and Security agenda 1–15, 59–62, 73–80; conclusion 13–15; gendering UN peacebuilding 5–13; women in peacemaking 3–5

women in peace? 18–20

women as peace-brokers 51–3

Women Peacemakers Program 93

women as victims 7–8

women's agency 94–5

women's 'economic empowerment' 8–9

women's reflections on peacebuilding 46–58

women's role in peacebuilding 3–5

women's substantive peace 22–3

women's substantive representation 20–22

Wood, Elisabeth Jean 63, 67

working to include women's needs/interests 41–4

WPS agenda *see* Women, Peace and Security agenda

Zarkov, Dubravka 40